DEBUSSY AND WAGNER

DEBUSSY

AND

WAGNER

Robin Holloway

EULENBURG BOOKS
LONDON

Ernst Eulenburg Ltd
48 Great Marlborough Street
London W1V 2BN

ISBN 0 903873 26 5 paperback
ISBN 0 903873 25 7 hardback

Printed and bound in England by
Caligraving Ltd, Thetford, Norfolk

Cover design by John Brennan

CONTENTS

	Preface	7
	Notes on books and editions	10
I.	Introduction	12
II.	Some early works	22
III.	Theory of Opera	50
IV.	*Pelléas* and Tristan	60
V.	The Interludes in *Pelléas*	76
VI.	Wagnerian minutiae in *Pelléas*	96
VII.	*Le Martyre de Saint Sébastien*	143
VIII.	*Jeux*	160
IX.	Conjunction	195

to Jehane

PREFACE

My view of the relation between Debussy and Wagner has some amusing precursors, including Richard Strauss, who remarked during a 1907 performance of *Pelléas* ' but all that is *Parsifal* ', and Cocteau, writing in *Le Coq et l'Arlequin* of 'the dense fog pierced by the lightnings of Bayreuth' that 'turns into a light snowy mist flecked by the impressionistic sun'. But on the whole the orthodoxy has been that, while there are obvious traces in his early works of Debussy's early enthusiasm for Wagner, the music of his maturity complements his later hostile attitude in its complete purgation of all Wagnerian traits. Debussy has been taken, especially by his compatriots, as pre-eminently the anti-Wagnerian composer, restoring lucidity, moderation and restraint after the long centuries of foreign sway in which Wagner was the last and cruellest tyrant. An attitude so disinterested as Koechlin's has been rare. 'It is not absurd' he wrote ' to think that Wagnerian influence on Claude Debussy was fruitful. It is a fact that true geniuses, and particularly French ones, use foreign influences in order to broaden their own natures.' More recently, thanks largely to the biographical researches of Edward Lockspeiser, Debussy's continued pre-occupation with Wagner throughout his maturity has become firmly established; indeed something of a commonplace.

But if there are connections of ethos and spirit, there are likely to be musical connections too. I take it to be axiomatic that what is well-loved in youth never disappears when the man puts away childish things; it is *always* present in some form or other, however wayward or submerged. Wagner got Debussy young enough for this to be inevitably true. Where the connections are, how they work, what they mean; this is what I attempt, by analysis and commentary part technical part literary, wholly interpretative, to show; demonstrating in particular works of Debussy a complex of Wagnerian reminiscence both in music and of subject-matter which eventually compels the proposition that, whether or not he re-presents an extreme reaction against Wagnerism, Debussy can be more completely understood as one of its most characteristic products.

7

Perhaps it would be better to say straight out what I say at the end of the first chapter and again, with more substantiation, at the end of the last; that, within the limits of a subtle and specialized relationship, Debussy must be recognized as the most profoundly Wagnerian of all composers. For I use the word 'characteristic' not to .mean, as it would of Wagner's German heirs, 'characteristic of Wagner', but on the contrary, 'characteristic of Debussy'. Debussy's genius is one of the most original in the history of the art, and insistence upon his debt to Wagner clearly does not suggest the continuity with Wagnerian music and matter that can be seen in *Guntram*, say., or the *Gurrelieder;* and thence at varying removes, in *Elektra* and *Die Glückliche Hand,* in *Der Ägyptische Helena* and *Moses und Aron,* in *Metamorphosen* and the *Modern Psalms.* In Debussy the influence of Wagner is already oblique when most direct; as his style retreats into its characteristic originality, Wagnerian traces so comparatively palpable as those of *La Damoiselle élue* and the *Cinq Poèmes de Charles Baudelaire* are thinned and relinquished. In *Pelléas* there is a subterranean commentary of subtly-transformed reminiscences of and associations with Wagnerian sources; and in *Jeux* (where the investigation ends) a Wagnerian influence so completely assimilated that merely stylistic indications of it are hardly to be seen. Nevertheless, Wagner remains at work deep within this music; and this raises questions as to the meaning of Wagner's participation in the process by which Debussy attained his radicality.

Such a deliberately partial angle can nowhere pretend to comprehensiveness; and important aspects of both composers go barely touched on or entirely unmentioned. The concern is limited by the title – Debussy under his Wagnerian aspect, or the area in which the two composers overlap. I find encouragement for this venture in words which should perhaps be taken as admonitory. 'Meaningless resemblances between composers can be found wherever sought for. Until we know how the details work and to what purpose, comprehension can only be not simply provisional (for that is what it is at best), but illusory.' Charles Rosen's remarks (taken very much out of context, and first read well after I'd finished this book) give a better brief indication of my intention than I can myself. I find the connection between Debussy and Wagner not meaningless; I attempt to show how the details work; and trust

Preface

that the way I interpret them to find a meaning is not simply illusory — nor, for that matter, simply provisional!

My thanks are due to the late Egon Wellesz who by his contempt for the whole project first stirred me into thinking for myself; to Philip Radcliffe, kindest and most solicitous of supervisors; to Derrick Puffett for constant stimulation and encouragement; to Richard Langham-Smith for some corrections (no doubt there will be moɪe); and to Sir William Glock, whose stringent regard for verbal nicety has superintended the conversion from thesis to book. Also to the various foundations under whose auspices or with whose help this work was begun, continued, and finished — New College Oxford, King's College Cambridge, and Gonville & Caius College Cambridge.

R.H.

Cambridge
November 1978

NOTES ON BOOKS & EDITIONS

I have kept footnotes and references to a minimum, and mention here rather than in the text the books which I have used for background. For Debussy's journalism I have gone of course to *Monsieur Croche the Dilettante-Hater* as reprinted by Dover (1962) in *Three Classics in the Aesthetic of Music*. It has been supplemented occasionally by Vallas's *The Theories of Claude Debussy* (Dover 1967) — a title as factitious as the contents are naïve. Richard Langham-Smith of the University of Lancaster has prepared a more complete edition of Debussy's writings which will no doubt throw up some interesting new things.[1] Lockspeiser's one-volume *Debussy* in the Master Musicians series (Dent) is by no means superseded by his two-volume *Debussy: his Life & Work* (Cassell); I have used both to sketch the background to *Le Martyre de S. Sébastien* and to *Jeux*, as well as the entirely introductory Chapter I. The Nietzsche works referred to here are *The Case of Wagner* and *Nietzsche contra Wagner*. Herbert Eimert's article on *Jeux* is in *Die Reihe*, volume 5.

The editions of music used are as follows:

Wagner
> *Tristan und Isolde*
> Vocal score by Karl Klindworth, English translation by Frederick Jameson; published by Schott, copyright 1906.
> Miniature score published by Eulenburg.
> *Parsifal*
> Vocal score by Klindworth, English by Margaret Glyn; published by Schott, copyright 1902.
> Miniature score published by Eulenburg.

Debussy
> *La Damoiselle élue:* v.s. and m.s.
> *Cinq Poèmes de Charles Baudelaire.*
> *Pelléas et Mélisande:* v.s. and m.s.
> *Le Martyre de Saint Sébastien* v.s. (m.s. of "Symphonic Fragments").
> *Jeux:* piano score and m.s.

All these works are used in the standard editions published by Durand.

1. Secker and Warburg, 1977.

Books and Editions

Ariettes Oubliées
Chansons de Bilitis
Proses Lyriques
These are referred to in the standard editions published by Jobert.

CHAPTER I

Introduction

1. *Wagner in France*

And as to Richard Wagner, it is obvious, it is glaringly obvious,
that Paris is the very soil for him: the more French music
adapts itself to the needs of the *âme moderne* the more
Wagnerian will it become.

Nietzsche contra Wagner

Wagner's influence upon the French *fin de siècle* is a complex
and fascinating subject which cannot be investigated here. A total
misunderstanding of his achievement transforms him into something quite other than his real self; the Wagner to whom Mallarmé's
Hommage is appropriate is as much an indigenous invention as
Baudelaire's Edgar Allen Poe. Above all he is divested of his
quintessential German-ness; he is no longer sublime and massive,
no longer mythological, regenerative, didactic. The most characteristic Wagnerism in France is an affair of *frissons* and *parfums,*
swoonings and strangeness, 'triumphant revels' as Mallarmé says—
in Nietzsche's words, 'all that thrills, of extravagant caresses, of all
the femininity from the vocabulary of happiness.'

Some French musicians were so overcome by Wagnerism that
their entire career passed in a perpetual vacillation towards and
against the alien allegiance. Three composers in particular require
notice because their reactions offer varying parallels and contrasts
to those of Debussy; they are Chabrier, Chausson and d'Indy. In
1869 d'Indy heard *Das Rheingold* and *Tristan* at Munich, returning
in 1870 for *Die Walküre.* He was also among the French contingent
at the first Bayreuth festival in 1876. In 1879 Chabrier, aged 38,
travelled to Munich at the instance of Duparc to hear *Tristan,* from
which he emerged saying 'There is enough music for a century in
this work; the man has left us nothing more to do.' Chausson,
aged 24, heard Wagner in Munich that summer too; there again for
Tristan in 1880, he wrote 'I know of no other work possessing

such intensity of feeling.' When *Parsifal* received its first performance in 1882, Chausson and d'Indy were at Bayreuth among the enthusiasts. Debussy was there for the first time in 1888, aged 26; and he returned again the year after.

Of course Chabrier still found something to do after his Wagnerian *bouleversement*. For the rest of his life he ranged between the popular style of which he is such a master, and his several attempts at Wagnerian music-drama on heroic subjects. The first, *Gwendoline*, was finished in 1886; *Briséis*, the most ambitious, was incomplete at his death in 1894. This vacillation, between the natural bent of his genius and his passion for a genre so decidedly out of his range, appears to have contributed to his mental breakdown and premature death. Chausson's enthusiasm was not so unfortunate. Already in 1884 in his unfinished *Hélène* he was trying in vain 'to avoid being too Wagnerian'. In the ten years from 1885 that he devoted to his opera *Le Roi Arthus,* his attitude to his presiding deity moderated somewhat. A composer deriving his own libretto from Celtic romance and legend must almost inevitably incur resemblance to and comparison with *Tristan.* Though he wrote of 'that frightful Wagner who is blocking my path', he did not, unlike his friend Debussy, abandon the faith; his further remarks on Wagner could stand as an epitaph to Chabrier's and his own misguided labours:

> When a genius as powerful, as dominating as Richard Wagner appears in the world, he gives off so much splendour that after him there follows a kind of darkness . . . hence general uncertainty, gropings, attempts in all directions in order to try to escape from the crushing glory which seems to obstruct every road.

Chausson's accidental death, not before he had realized his talent in some exquisite songs, at least brought relief. D'Indy however did not require it. Aged 25, he had vowed (upon seeing the first complete *Ring* in 1876) that he would lead the movement to establish a French music-drama. 'The ardent idealism of his nature', writes Martin Cooper, 'combined with a strong taste for the imposing and magnificent, his religious faith and his passion for rich and solid musical structure made it inevitable that Wagner should be his inspiration when he came to write for the theatre.' But d'Indy's *actions musicaux* creak and labour; the response to Wagner that fabricates in his shadow vague elevated allegories is one that goes counter to the French musical spirit. Massenet, using a few superficial Wagnerisms to add piquancy to his erotic vocabulary, was truer to his own and his national character, while Fauré seems with calm disinterest to abjure the whole vexed question; as Koechlin said of the imaginary forest in the *Ballade,* 'we are assured that Fauré had that of *Siegfried* in mind; but without Mime, Siegfried, Wotan, or the dragon – and without Wagner . . .'

Debussy seems to have been the only Wagnerite among French composers who felt some monitory intuition about the dangers of the infatuation. Though his attitude to Wagner, ranging as it did from early devotion to later hostility, was unbalanced in both directions, in his music he is the one composer who, neither resisting Wagner's sway nor succumbing slavishly to it, eventually produces music which while it is extraordinarily original and masterly in its own terms, could none the less not have existed were it not for Wagner's example.

Debussy's views of the three composers who offer some sort of parallel to his own attitude, casually expressed though they are in letters and journalism, show how his superior intuition protected him. From a letter to Chausson of 1893; 'One thing I would like to see you lose is your pre-occupation with undertones; I believe we have been led into that by the same old R. Wagner, and that we think too often about the frame before having the picture, and sometimes the richness of the latter makes us pass over the poverty of the idea.' About Chabrier he has less cause to adopt a tactful tone; having deplored that this composer 'so marvellously endowed by the comic muse' should have attempted flights beyond his powers, he goes on to say that Chabrier 'died in the pursuit of the lyrical drama – that Glucko-Wagnerian importation so foreign to our genius.' Finally, behind the respectful attention given to D'Indy's *Fervaal* and *L'Etranger* one can sense a distinct lack of enthusiasm; when Debussy's praise is sincere his vocabulary, his style altogether, is very different. However, disapproval becomes patent when he says 'the idea of compelling the symphonic development to depend on the dramatic action was but a device, which never proved of much service except to Wagner and German thought.'

2. *Hostility to Wagner — Nietzsche and Debussy*

The earliest hostility to Wagner and his works came from outraged conservatism or outraged propriety. Earlier detractors failed to understand Wagner's greatness. Nietzsche's hostility was different; he understood Wagner all too well. Yet 'he who wakes us always wounds us' — Wagner with all his 'fog' and 'disease' remained the crucial episode in Nietzsche's intellectual growth, the vital force, enlightening even in the very rejection by which he discovered his true position.

Mutatis mutandis the similarity of Nietzsche's and Debussy's reactions to Wagner is notable. Debussy also was infatuated in youth, and for him too increasing doubts grew through resentment into detestation. Behind this stands fear: an old-guard anti-Wagnerian like Hanslick hated Wagner for his assault upon the classical virtues; Nietzsche and Debussy, 'avant-garde' Wagnerians, hated him for his assault upon themselves. Wagner looms too close, overwhelming those who submit to his dangerous lures. Nietzsche speaks of Wagner's 'art of seduction', Debussy of 'the impure art of Wagner, with its peculiar beauty and seduction'. They both refer to him continually, particularly when *Parsifal* is mentioned, as 'the old magician . . . sorcerer . . . Klingsor . . . poisoner . . . conjuror . . .'. They would unmask this conjuror's tricks, but have already revealed in the intensity of their wish the extent to which the tricks are effectual. 'If he had been a little more human', Debussy writes, 'he would be great for all time.' Nietzsche goes further; for him Wagner is corruption itself:- 'Is Wagner a man at all? Is he not rather a disease? Everything he touches he contaminates. He has made music sick.'

Wagner sways the unwilling will: 'gigantic forces lie concealed in it; it drives one beyond its own domain' says Nietzsche, and Debussy, 'it is worse than obsession. It is possession. You no longer belong to yourself.' Their metaphors come from grand natural phenomena: Nietzsche speaks of 'lava which blocks its own course by congealing' and compares the 'endless melody' to entering the sea — 'gradually one loses one's footing and one ultimately abandons oneself to the mercy or fury of the elements: one has to swim.' Debussy also finds the *Ring* 'irresistible as the sea', and believes Wagnerians to be 'blinded by the last rays of this setting sun'. At times they lapse into absurdity — in Nietzsche's contention that Wagner's music when disassociated from the theatre 'is simply bad music, perhaps the worst that has ever been composed' — in Debussy's description of Amfortas as a whining shop-girl, or his suggestion that seeing the *Ring* one sees the same opera four times over. Their differences, too, are revealing. Nietzsche develops the idea of sickness and moral depravity, which he associates with Wagner's powers of intoxicating rhetoric and his lack of lucidity. In a famous passage he summons his ideal . . . 'what we halcyonians miss in Wagner . . . *la gaya scienza* . . . light feet, wit, fire, grave grand logic, stellar dancing, wanton intellectuality, the vibrating. light of the south, the calm sea — perfection . . .' Debussy's denunciations, by contrast, tend to collapse into limp extravagance:-

> Wagner's work suggests a striking picture; Bach as the Holy Grail, Wagner as Klingsor wishing to crush the Grail and usurp its place . . . Bach shines supreme over music, and in his goodness he has reserved for our hearing words as yet unknown, of the great lesson he has bequeathed us of disinterested love of music. Wagner disappears into the background . . . he is fading away . . . a black, disturbing shadow.

Wagner here is transformed from Klingsor to become a fairy-tale monster like his own Alberich. But ironically enough, Alberich's last words as he disappears from the *Ring*, are 'Sei treu!' Debussy's parallel rebounds; Wagner recedes, but his reluctant son remains true in spite of himself, indeed without really knowing it.

Both Nietzsche and Debussy owe more to Wagner, as the source of their most important self-discovery, than to any other influence. They are both afraid of the 'too huge Godhead', and reluctant to acknowledge it; they mock or denounce with hectic exhilaration, to show, unconvincingly, that the 'subtle poison' has not turned their head. Nietzsche's later dealings with Wagner oscillate between a vivid apprehension, usually in his correspondence, of Wagner's 'extraordinary sublimity of feeling, something experienced in the very depths of music . . .', and the bad faith with which he customarily treated these apprehensions in his published writings. Debussy's uncertainty, altogether less deeply-grounded, is none the less similar, and there is the same anxiety to conceal the extent of Wagner's encroachment. 'One glimpses here and there' remarks Vallas naively 'that he never ceased to cherish a real affection for

Tristan und Isolde.' The complex ambiguity of his attitude towards *Parsifal* will be discussed in due course. Moreover his hostility to Wagner is (except in the *Golliwogg's Cake Walk*) entirely verbal; musically he remained a follower of Wagner, though in devious manner, for the rest of his life.

3. *Wagner as Miniaturist*

The final point of resemblance between Nietzsche and Debussy's view of Wagner is also the most interesting. They both appear to have had a perverse idea of Wagner as a *miniaturist*. Perverse because Wagner's supreme mastery is shown above all in his control of a long paragraph of continuous music; in the way that detail is both allowed to blossom on its own account, yet always perfectly to take its place in larger structures which balance to make a complete act. But for Nietzsche this was not so: 'Everywhere paralysis, distress and numbness, or hostility and chaos; both striking one with ever-increasing force the higher the forms of organization are into which one ascends. The whole no longer lives at all; it is composed, reckoned up, artificial, a fictitious thing'. For him, Wagner 'is really only worthy of admiration and love by virtue of his inventiveness in small things, in his elaboration of details – here one is quite justified in proclaiming him a master of the first rank, as our greatest musical *miniaturist*, who compresses an infinity of meaning and sweetness into the smallest space'.

It seems to me that Debussy also must have heard Wagner like this, though of course this is impossible to prove. The characteristically French enjoyment of Wagner which involves hearing his music as *frissons* and *parfums* would necessarily preclude the possibility of grasping his mastery of large-scale forms. Moreover Debussy's conception of how music should be shaped opposes itself, even in his writings, to the Wagnerian grandeur of proportion. He says of Mussorgsky, 'the form is so varied that by no possibility whatever can it be related to any established, one might say official form, since it depends on and is made up of *successive minute touches mysteriously linked together by means of an instinctive clairvoyance*'. And, complimenting Rameau, he regrets that French music should ever lose sight of *'that clarity of expression, that terse and condensed form,* which is the peculiar and significant quality of the French genius.' These remarks (my italics) are valuable for what they reveal of his personal ideal of composition; it is impossible to reconcile such an ideal with any view of Wagner, however appreciative, except one that hears him as a miniaturist who compresses 'an infinity of meaning and sweetness into the smallest space'. The same paradox is seen when he finds grudging praise for *Tristan* because in 'the swirl and passion of the music' he can descry 'the entrancing spirit of Chopin'. The odd feeling grows, that Nietzsche's words describe Debussy better than they do any other composer. The continuation of the quotation about Wagner as above all a miniaturist should make this clear: 'His wealth of colour, of chiaroscuro, of the mystery of a dying light, so pampers our senses that afterwards almost every other musician strikes us as being too robust.' And a passage follows soon after in *The Case of Wagner* that curiously anticipates what will become Debussy's actual practice in some of his works . . . 'a lexicon of Wagner's most intimate phrases — a host of short fragments of from five to fifteen bars each, of music which *nobody knows* . . .'.

4. *Debussy and Wagner*

Debussy was a Wagnerite before his visits to Bayreuth in 1888 and 1889. His first introduction had been in his teens at the Paris Conservatoire; he and his teacher Lavignac went together through the *Tannhäuser* overture, at a time when Wagner's music was still beyond the pale, the province of bohemians and *apaches*. 'The experience must have been overwhelming' says Lockspeiser. 'The young professor and his eager pupil became so absorbed in the novel Wagnerian harmonics that they forgot all sense of time. When they eventually decided to leave they found themselves locked in and were obliged to grope their way out, arm in arm, down the rickety stairs and the dark corridors of the crumbling scholastic building.'

At the Villa Medici where he proceeded in 1885 to take up the *Prix de Rome*, Debussy quarrelled with Hébert, the director, over various matters, Wagner being one. In later life he recalled it thus:

'Hébert loved music passionately but Wagner's music not at all. At that time I was a Wagnerian to the pitch of forgetting the simplest rules of courtesy.' He continues, with a blandness not often found in his utterances on this subject, 'nor did I imagine that I could ever come almost to agree with this enthusiastic old man who had travelled through all these emotions with his eyes open, whereas we hardly grasped their meaning or how to use them'. There are two interesting points here — first the suggestion that enthusiasm for Wagner is necessarily callow, something that the man of experience and maturity will inevitably outgrow; and second, the 'almost', which begs every question by conveying a reluctant admission that this youthful habit can sometimes recur.

'1889! Delightful period when I was madly Wagnerian' (he wrote in 1903); it lasted from the late 'eighties until about the middle of the 'nineties, gradually cooling into the more familiar disenchantment. He attended the Paris *Lohengrin* of 1887, which can be taken as the first round in the most fervent phase of French Wagnerism. The next two summers gave him his Bayreuth experience of *Tristan, Parsifal*, and *Die Meistersinger*. In 1893 he heard *Lohengrin* again at the Opéra; took part as one of the two pianists in the introduction to Paris of *Das Rheingold;* and saw the first French staging of *Die Walküre*. In February 1894 he earned 1,000 francs for playing and singing Act I of *Parsifal* to a private gathering. In addition, the orchestral concerts of these years often included bleeding chunks, after which Debussy would ostentatiously leave the hall.

His account of his disenchantment was written some years later. 'After several years of passionate pilgrimage to Bayreuth, I began to entertain doubts as to the Wagnerian formula; or rather, it seemed to me that it could serve only the particular case of Wagner's genius.' So far unexceptionable; but he continues. 'He was a great collector of formulae. He assembled them all into one, which appears individual to those who are ill-acquainted with music.' After a comparison of Wagner 'without denying his genius' to Victor Hugo, he concludes, 'The thing, then, was to find *what came after Wagner's time but not after Wagner's manner.'* The phrase I italicize shows the same instinct for self-protection that had enabled him to comment so shrewdly upon the Wagnerian failures of Chabrier, Chausson, and d'Indy. However, it is the perversity, and sometimes sheer silliness, suggested by the middle of the remarks quoted, that predominates from now on in his utterances on the subject. Most of them were made when he saw his first complete *Ring* in London, April 1903. Whatever he felt constrained to write, the experience was overwhelming – as Lockspeiser says, he writes 'with a certain undertone of bitterness, even terror.' The focal remark in these notices is not injudicious: 'One does not criticize a work of such magnitude as the *Ring* . . . its too sumptuous greatness renders futile the legitimate desire to grasp its proportions' – the 'miniaturist' view again. There is no chance, with a response that can call Wagner 'as irresistible as the sea', of its victim avoiding Wagner's impact; but equally with such determined detachment as Debussy otherwise shows, there is little danger of drowning.

After this Debussy's attitudes do not change, but simply refine upon the same ambiguous feeling that could produce now some withering sarcasm, and now cause him to leave a performance of *Tristan* 'literally shaking with emotion'. That was in 1914; he saw *Parsifal* too in that year, for the first time since the Bayreuth visit of 1889. His notice produced a puerile account of the plot, calling Klingsor 'the finest character' and so forth. That this is merely defensive becomes clear when he confesses that these remarks apply only to Wagner the poet, and 'have nothing to do with the musical beauty of the opera, which is supreme. It is incomparable and bewildering, splendid and strong. *Parsifal* is one of the loveliest monuments of sound ever raised to the serene glory of music.' This tribute is achieved at the expense of a perversity – *Parsifal* is 'an admirable proof of the futility of formulae – a magnificent contradiction of the *Ring*.' But it is generous; and its significance is paramount for some of Debussy's greatest music.

5. *Conclusion*

The truth is, that of all the French composers influenced by the aesthetic and the music of Wagner, Debussy's response was the most far-reaching. His career, though it is littered at all times with uncompleted projects, produces no such Wagnerian fatalities as a *Gwendoline* or a *Roi Arthus*. He passed through a mere 'delightful period' of youthful fervour, which he later disavowed as a callow and temporary phase. Or rather, he passed from such a period not into disillusion and hatred lit up by occasional flashes of involuntary enthusiasm, as his *writings* would have us believe; but, as his *music* shows, into a period of mature openness to Wagner's influence, an influence that become subtly more potent as he grew older, but which by no means inhibited the individuality of his idiosyncratic genius. Rather, indeed, was it the means by which his originality came to its richest flowering.

That Wagner is the most profound influence in Debussy's life and music is still insufficiently recognized. It is Mussorgsky and the other Russians whose hold is temporary; Wagner never let him go. How he found in the minutiae of Wagner's music all kinds of hints for his own, it is my purpose to demonstrate, evoking as exemplar Wölfflin's ideal of a method which can trace the development from painter to painter by comparing 'hand with hand, cloud with cloud, twig with twig, down to the grain of the wood.' Wölfflin asserted that it was in the *miniature* — the small decorative arts, the lines of ornament, etc., that 'the feeling of form satisfies itself in the purest way, and it is here that the birthplace of a new style must be sought.'

I want, by applying something analogous to the moments of Debussy's music that require it, to try to ascertain *how* Wagner's music appealed to him as compressing 'an infinity of meaning and sweetness into the smallest space'; *what* was his 'lexicon of Wagner's most intimate phrases', his 'host of short fragments of from five to fifteen bars'; and *where* he was most pampered by its 'wealth of colour, of chiaroscuro, of the mystery of a dying light': and *why*. More simply, I want to show just how much Wagner there actually is in Debussy. By establishing these things, it is possible to see just how far Wagner penetrates into the essence of Debussy's peculiarity, and yet how that peculiarity transforms him into something completely new. Debussy could never be called the musical heir of Wagner; but he must be recognized to be, within the limits of a subtle and specialized relationship, the most profoundly Wagnerian of all composers.

CHAPTER II

SOME EARLY WORKS

1. *La Damoiselle élue*

Debussy began *La Damoiselle élue* in 1887 and completed it in 1889. In 1888 he visited Bayreuth for the first time, for *Parsifal* and *Die Meistersinger;* in 1889 he returned for these two again and added to them *Tristan*. It is not surprising, especially in the context of his youthful Wagnerism, that the work is permeated with Wagnerian echoes and reminiscences.

Even where they can be directly compared, in their re-creation of an idealized medievalry, Wagner and the pre-Raphaelites have nothing in common in aesthetic means or in essential interests. Occasionally however, and peripherally, they can reach from their different sources towards something of the same effect. This is most apparent in *Tristan* and *Parsifal*, with their Romance stories and fusion of fleshly and spiritual elements. Some of the stage-directions in *Parsifal* even suggest a visual correspondence; for instance the 'rose-lipp'd garden of girls' in Act II - 'the magic garden fills the stage with tropical vegetation and luxuriant growth of flowers . . . from all sides rush in the flower-maidens, clad in light veil-like garments . . . they seem as though just startled out of sleep'. And again, the 'dazzling ray of light' shed on the Grail in Act I, 'glowing ever deeper, a shining wine-purple colour'. The first brings to mind innumerable barely-differentiated Burne-Joneses of bare undifferentiated girls, the second resembles Rossetti in his mode of opulent mysticism.

Debussy was attracted to *The Blessed Damozel* as a contrast with Wagner. In fact his setting takes its colour from tendencies in Wagner that are entirely compatible with pre-Raphaelite themes as they became diffused and commonplace; yet at the same time it reveals an intuitive accord with the Brotherhood's earliest ideal of sweet austerity. Rossetti's Damozel, offered as a vision of exquisite poignancy, is blowsy and saccharine in realization. Debussy renders with perfect success the chaste simplicity intended by the poem;

he has learnt the means from the appropriate music in *Parsifal*.

The relation of *La Damoiselle* to *Parsifal* as a whole, is analogous to its relation to Rossetti's original. Not, of course, that *Parsifal* is blowsy or saccharine! Simply that, in deriving inspiration from *Parsifal*'s treatment of subject-matter close to *La Damoiselle*, Debussy has no taste for and no need for *Parsifal*'s troubling depths. In avoiding serious involvement with the central core of *Parsifal* he also avoids the temptation to bring out the mawkish undercurrents of Rossetti's poem (and indeed has relinquished the means). His 'genius for good taste' is shown already in his ability so delicately to waive the possibilities either of depth or of mawkishness; they are kept latent, and it comes as something of a shock to re-read the poem in English and feel anew its crudity, or to think back from *La Damoiselle* to Kundry and the flower-maidens, and then to re-place them in their context. Rossetti is transcended and restored to his intention; *Parsifal* is relieved of its gloomy profundity, and only the sweetness of its religious, and the *pudeur* of its erotic aspects, are retained. The depiction of Amfortas, of Kundry in Klingsor's grip, of Parsifal's growth from foolishness to wisdom Debussy leaves virtually untouched; when their presence is occasionally heard, they too are lightened in the service of sensuous delight.

La Damoiselle élue abounds in echoes and reminiscences of Debussy's contemporary experience of Wagner at Bayreuth and at home. *Parsifal* declares itself almost at once. Wagner opens with a slow intensely-charged unison theme, that is then repeated amidst a haze of diaphanous arpeggii and rhythmically ambiguous chords, disappearing on a high sustained triad into the empyrean, the whole statement[1] taking 19 bars of a very slow tempo. Debussy opens with a pattern of chords whose function during the work proves to be rather as an ostinato than thematic, and has reached a high sustained triad through a rustle of string arpeggii in only two further bars - Ex. 1. Wagner immediately balances his vast opening statement in another 19 bars, the theme now in the minor and given sharper rhythmic and instrumental articulation[2]. Debussy's next 4 bars, though different in keys and decorative detail, are also essentially there to balance the first 4. Already, then, Debussy's

1. *Parsifal* m.s. pp. 1-8.
2. Ibid., pp. 8-15.

use of a Wagnerian original indicates something of the relation between the two composers' different aims. Debussy reproduces the opening of *Parsifal* as two wafts of sonority, rather than a dual presentation of a theme; 'and his version is briefer, lighter and more evanescent.

After the first announcement of the Dresden Amen the *Parsifal* prelude moves into $\frac{6}{4}$. Debussy's next section is also in $\frac{6}{4}$, and though the resemblance (to the gentler rather than the brassier bars

Ex. 1   Opening of *La Damoiselle Elue*

of the original) is principally one of mood, the motif of a descending scale, as well as their identical place in the work's unfolding, is common to both - see Ex. 2. The next reminiscence is slightly

Ex. 2a *Parsifal*, v.s., p. 5

Ex. 2b *La Damoiselle*, v.s., p. 4

25

harder to establish. A passage of 4 bars in *La Damoiselle* - Ex. 3b - appears to echo a peculiarly memorable passage in *Parsifal* Act I, where Gurnemanz described the flight of the mate of the swan the callow youth has just shot down. At one point - Ex. 3a - the Dresden Amen is incorporated into the swan-motif (originally from *Lohengrin*). Debussy seems here to be unconsciously recalling this focal point of the whole lovely episode; moreover it is immediately played again a fourth higher. The melodic contour and harmony is similar, and the figuration on divided violins gives the same airborne effect. While du côté de chez *Parsifal's* swan, I think it at least possible that the use of the original motif from *Lohengrin* has left its trace on the harmony and movement of the Damozel's central aria (which is given at a later appearance when both music and words[1] are closest to the original) - see Ex. 4.

The next example from *La Damoiselle* accompanies the chorus

Ex. 3a The Swan combined with the 'Dresden' (*Parsifal*, v.s., p.51)

1. a) "Seeking his wife he flew up with her [to circle over the lake]."

    b) "We two . . . will seek the groves
        Where the lady Mary is . . ."

Ex. 3b   *La Damoiselle*, v.s., p. 7 (no key-signature in m.s.)

Ex. 4a   *Parsifal*, v.s., p. 50 (harp omitted)

Ex. 4b *La Damoiselle*, v.s., pp. 18-19

singing of the souls of lovers, newly reunited, mounting past her to God 'comme de fines flammes' - Ex. 5a. This progression, especially in its doubling back on itself before advancing, recalls one always associated in *Parsifal* with the glowing of the Grail; Ex. 5b gives three instances. The usage, though similar in sound, is not the same; Debussy's triads being from minor to major, a minor third

Ex. 5a   *La Damoiselle*, v.s., p. 10 (harps omitted)

Ex. 5b i   *Parsifal*, v.s., p. 91

Ex. 5b ii

1 bar

Ex. 5b iii *Parsifal*, v.s., p. 271

Ex. 5b iv *Parsifal*, v.s., p. 276 (harp and string arpeggii omitted)

apart; Wagner's being a major third apart and moving (apart from
the first part of b i) from major to minor. However, a later passage
from *La Damoiselle* passes through both motions in pleasing suc-
cession, as she sings of Our Lady's 'five handmaidens, whose
names/Are five sweet symphonies' - Ex. 5c. Here the movement
from F minor to D major exactly reproduces that from A minor to
F# major in 5a; and the movement from E major to C minor
reproduces Wagner's in all the examples grouped under 5b (again
excepting the first bar of i).

The 'dove descending' motif following so immediately after the
last of these unveilings of the Grail surely gives Debussy a hint of
his continuation in this example - compare the end of 5a and 5b iv
(and also the two passages of Ex. 2). Debussy's very next bars - Ex.
6b - as so often in this work steer the whole phrase onto a 'floating'
ninth. As a student at the Conservatoire he used to shock his elders

Ex. 5c   *La Damoiselle*, v.s., p. 19

Ex. 6a   *Parsifal*, v.s., pp. 244-5

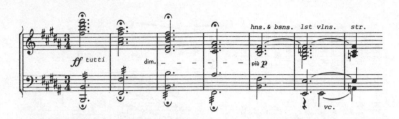

Ex. 6b   *La Damoiselle*, v.s., p. 10

and titivate his contemporaries by playing strings of unresolved ninths. 'Mon plaisir' was his justification - and indeed the delight he took in parallel ninths is evident throughout the work of his maturity. In *La Damoiselle* it is this chord that, one way and another, dominates the overall harmonic feel and gives the work its quintessential flavour. But so early as this the delight is still relatively subservient to tonal function and onward harmonic movement. This ninth, for instance, compromises between a moment of static pleasure and a forward motion by means of an F# pedal, successively the tonic of F# major (in 5a), the dominant of B major, the 9th on E, and the third of D. Such a movement recalls one of the great cornerstones of *Parsifal* both in its story and its musical architecture, Parsifal's Coronation in Act III. Here too the F# runs through the alternating tonic and dominant B major, quietens to become the 9th on E, and then converges from its echo in Debussy by lying suspended as an added 6th of A major as Parsifal performs his first humble office, baptism of the kneeling Kundry. I don't, however, care to press the fact that the words sung by the récitante over the E major 9th reached in 6a are 'Alors, elle s'inclina de nouveau . . .'

31

Ex. 7a   *La Damoiselle*, m.s., pp. 19-20

Ex. 7b   *Götterdämmerung*, m.s., pp. 90-92

One floating ninth will lead to another; the next example suggests a possible source in Wagner of a usage whose spirit - of an exhilarating harmonic dislocation - is the same even when its letter is not. Ex. 7a from *La Damoiselle* brings to mind a harmonic plunge characteristic of the *Götterdämmerung* love-duet - 7b; the connection will be clarified by also citing a passage from *Printemps* (Ex. 7c), one of Debussy's *envois de Rome*, written 1886-7. Ex. 7a plunges from a ninth on C in which B♭ is the 7th and E the 3rd, to one on F# where E becomes the 7th and B♭, now A#, becomes the 3rd. Brünnhilde 'remembering the flaming fire' plunges from the ninth on C to one on E, where the notes in common, though their function of course changes, are E and D. The passage from *Printemps* does just this, and is akin to the Wagner in its mood of

Ex. 7c   *Printemps*, m.s., pp. 58-60

elation, with fanfare motifs and whooping horns.[1] Perhaps one could say that the bars from *La Damoiselle* recall the bars from *Götterdämmerung* only through its cruder reproduction in *Printemps;* except that, apart from the syntactically exact reproduction of the harmonic shift, 7a is just as similar as 7c to 7b, but in different ways. They all mark the change with a toss of a scale; but 7a seems really to strain forward for its plunge as the Wagner does, and the plunge itself hits the new ninth fair and square, high and low, rather than as in 7c unveiling its notes in several steps. Even the 'wrong ninth' in 7a has three notes out of five in common with the 'right' one.

Ex. 8a   *Parsifal*, v.s., p. 159

Ex. 8b   *La Damoiselle*, v.s., p. 16

Another, looser, possible echo is given in Ex. 8; a generalized premonition (in harmony, melodic curve, orchestration) of the girl-garden in *Parsifal* which is destined to play so important a part in Debussy's relation to Wagner. But the next example is altogether different. The vision of the Damozel, lilies lying along her arm as if asleep, seems to send Debussy to his own pre-Raphaelite

1. Amusingly enough the magic fire, whose music does not recur as Brünnhilde recalls it, flickers up unmistakably within a few bars of this example from *Printemps* (m.s. pp. 62-3).

version of Isolde - see Ex. 9. Like the much more explicit reworking of the opening of *Tristan* in the fourth of the Baudelaire songs, the resolution of this harmonic impasse is completely un-Wagnerian.[1]

Ex. 9   *La Damoiselle*, v.s., p. 11

Ex. 10a   *Parsifal*, v.s., pp. 225-6

Ex. 10b   *La Damoiselle*, v.s., pp. 13-14

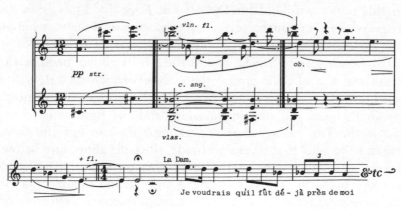

---

1. See the discussion of Ex. 15 below.

Parsifal soon returns; an interesting reminiscence since it is at the same time so characteristic of the more mature Debussy. This 'entry of the Damozel' (Ex. 10b) has the delicate waywardness of the musical characterization of Mélisande; and yet it would appear to derive from one of the most solemn moments in *Parsifal* - the hero's return near the beginning of Act III when, rebuked for wearing armour in holy ground on Good Friday, he disarms and is revealed at last as his true self. Wagner at the revelation of his Redeemer and Debussy at the first plaintive words of a long-throated Damozel - the one a moment of nerve-racking sublimity, the other of enchanting wistfulness. Ex. 1 has already shown this relation between the massy depth of the original and the lighter, even a trifle vapid, delicacy of its reflection. A recreation at once more profound and closer to the source can be seen in Ch. VI Ex. 6. In the earlier work, comparison would be odious.

Now the relation to the magic garden becomes more specific. Ex. 11b presents the same idea four times, in two pairs, the second the same as the first, a major 3rd lower and rescored. This single idea from *La Damoiselle* contains in little space a compression of several reminiscences of the flower maidens. The passage it recalls most immediately is Gurnemanz's description of the garden, with its foretaste of rich later material, during his Act I narration. This is appropriate because the glancing use in *La Damoiselle* of material from the flowermaidens is in itself a foretaste of the rich fascination this music will hold for Debussy in *Jeux*. Ex 11a i gives the passage where Gurnemanz tells of the 'garden of delight, wherein grow devilish lovely women'.[1] Three clarinets sway upwards in parallel first-inversion triads, a solo flute trills above; both at the bottom and top of their phrase the clarinets touch on a delicious major ninth. 11a ii comes a few bars later; the strings have the ninth (now in E♭) and the swaying motion, and the dominant trill is underneath. The passage from *La Damoiselle* also has the three clarinets in parallel first-inversion triads, the trills above and below, the turn in a lower key to the same idea on strings (Debussy's lower key being the same as Wagner's higher); and the harmony in each bar moves from its initial stable ninth to touch delicately on the dominant seventh a tritone away, with punning notes common to both chords.

1. '... teuflisch holde Frauen.'

Ex. 11a i *Parsifal*, v.s., p. 40

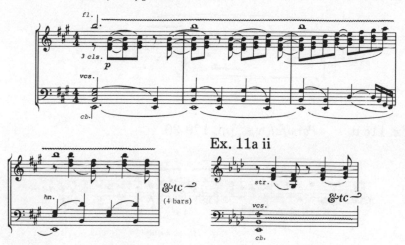

Ex. 11a ii

Ex. 11b *La Damoiselle*, v.s., p. 18

Ex. 11c i   *Parsifal*, v.s., p. 136

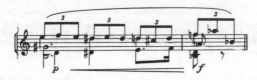

Ex. 11c ii   *Parsifal*, v.s., pp. 129-30

(three times)

Ex. 11d i   =   11b

Ex. 11d ii   =   11c ii (transposed up a 4th to correspond to 11d i)

And now from the foretaste to the fulfillment; 11c i gives the characteristic harmony of the flowermaidens as they first enter 'in a confused many-coloured throng'. This chord-pattern, essentially of two dominant sevenths a tritone apart, is used constantly, unchanged save for transposition, in shiftless irridescence throughout the flowermaid scene, and is finally absorbed into Kundry's wider spectrum of voluptuousness. I have quoted it from the most chromatic passage (v.s. pp. 135-8) where it rises by a semitone each bar; not quite at random in as much as this particular instance catches the wingéd joy at Debussy's pitch level (E-B♭ in the second pair of Ex. 11b). On its earlier appearances (pp. 129-30 - to very *Damoiselle*-like words — 'Wo find' ich den meinen? Wo ist mein

Geliebter?') it is in less of a rush, being repeated three times before sliding up a tone — see Ex. 11c ii; this repetition produces Debussy's effect of enclosing his move before moving again, while the unceasing blur of decoration in the Wagner is reduced in the Debussy to the little quintuplet turn. 11d condenses these moves to make their connection clearer.

Thus what amounts essentially to one bar of *La Damoiselle* can employ two widely-separated (though directly-connected) passages of *Parsifal* whose elements Debussy has rearranged and elided, to effect a ravishing glimpse into a new domain of pleasure. A still clearer reminiscence is found in the next example. Ex. 12a comes from the moment in *Parsifal* Act III where Gurnemanz rejoices over the return of the Spear. 12b is near the end of Amfortas's speech in the same act, where he imagines his dead father interceding on his behalf — 'Redeemer, give my son rest!' (They are both based on the work's opening motif). The melodic curve of Ex. 12c from *La Damoiselle* (which in fact is an extension of the end of Ex. 2b) follows 12b in its sequential repetition a major third lower. Harmonically, however, it makes the same acute and memorable step as 12a (see especially the third bar) and is at the same pitch.

Ex. 12a   *Parsifal*, v.s., p. 232

Ex. 12b   *Parsifal*, v.s., p. 263

Ex. 12c   *La Damoiselle*, v.s., p. 26

Ex. 13a   *Tristan*, bars 6-7 and 10-11

Ex. 13b   *Parsifal*, v.s., p. 238

Ex. 13c   *La Damoiselle*, v.s., p. 27

The last glimpse of the Damozel brings a reminiscence of the opening of *Tristan* which also strikingly recalls the same progression used where Gurnemanz indicates to Kundry that Parsifal should be annointed with no common water. The chords are the same, and at the same pitch, and the resemblance is increased by all three examples' pungent yet dulcet scoring for woodwind (Ex. 13). Finally, Ex. 14 gives the end of *Parsifal* Act I and of *La Damoiselle*.

Ex. 14a *Parsifal*, **end of Act 1**

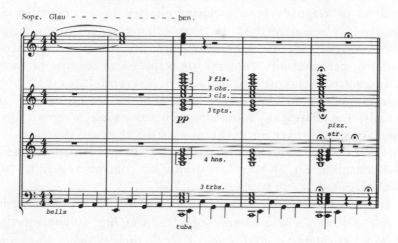

Ex. 14b **End of *La Damoiselle***

No great resemblance in itself — though note the triad of women's voices, and the position of horns, trumpets and trombones in the C major chords — but one that suitably rounds off the evidence.

Though *La Damoiselle élue* is clearly well-steeped in Debussy's contemporary Wagnerism, it can hardly be called Wagnerian in the usual sense — as *Guntram* is Wagnerian, for instance, or the *Gurrelieder*. This early but so characteristic work is 'Wagnerian' in a way that applies to Debussy rather than to Wagner. In *La Damoiselle* Debussy has remembered moments from Wagner for which his individual sensibility feels a particular predilection. This 'lexicon of Wagner's most intimate phrases' he incorporates into his own style and method, in every other respect quite different from Wagner. He is not commonly thought of as Wagnerian because, paradoxically enough, his response to specific moments in Wagner is so intense that he more or less reproduces them in his own composition; while at the same time he has no use for, and actually repudiates, any more comprehensive view. Wagner's direct successors took over an entire apparatus; they are the heirs to a tradition within which they continued their work of extension and consolidation. Debussy's response by contrast is private, fugitive, unrooted in any such continuity.

In style and in subject-matter *La Damoiselle* is the first of what I call 'Debussy's Wagnerian Works' — the line is continued in *Pelléas*, *Le Martyre*, and *Jeux*. To call these works 'Wagnerian' at all is at the same time to realize sharply the extent of Debussy's newness.

2. *Cinq Poèmes de Charles Baudelaire*

If *La Damoiselle élue* is impregnated with echoes of *Parsifal*, the five Baudelaire songs which belong to the same years (1887-9) complete the picture of Debussy's early Wagnerian works in their corresponding preoccupation with *Tristan und Isolde*.

However, these wonderful songs are somewhat outside the mainstream of Debussy's development. They are long and exceptionally rich in harmony, with nothing of the sparseness and brevity that characterizes the later and more typical songs. The complexity of such late works as the Mallarmé songs of 1913 is brought about by rapid changes of mood and texture that create a subtle and elliptical form. 'Developing' would be a misnomer in a description of this music, which has, moreover, somehow the capacity to suggest that for it to 'develop' would be indelicate, a pedantry destructive of its essence (which so far as the notes go is very simple). The complexity of the *Cinq Poèmes*, on the other hand, is that of many notes, a density of working-out. In this sense only they are the most complex music Debussy ever wrote, and it is here that he comes nearest to a traditionally Wagnerian fullness of motivic development.

Le Balcon, the first of the set, is the song which shows this uncharacteristic quality most explicitly. It is also uncharacteristic of Debussy in its forward-moving momentum; the opening pages in particular have an exuberance that brings to mind the Straussian *Schwung*. In this song there is no reminiscence of specific passages in Wagner. Rather it is a question of a total Wagnerian permeation of the harmony — as befits the rich intensity of the poem — and a Wagnerian motivic working and forward momentum. In this respect *Le Balcon* derives from those scenes in the Wagner operas where a leitmotif becomes an accompaniment, an omnipresent and fully-thematic support to a free vocal line, forming an overall structure at once rhapsodic and tightly-knit. Examples of this are Isolde's Narration in *Tristan* Act I, Wotan's farewell at the end of *Walküre,* and whole stretches of *Meistersinger* Act III. Closest in spirit to *Le Balcon* are the more reflective passages near the beginning of *Tristan* Act II as Isolde awaits her lover (for example, v.s. pp. 138-40; 145-9; 152-9). The exceptionally complicated piano part in the Debussy has very much the feel (and to a certain extent the sound) of an orchestral transcription; the texture it most closely resembles is of these pages in the piano-score of *Tristan*.

Baudelaire's *Le Balcon* consists of six stanzas in each of which the first and last lines are identical. Debussy mirrors this device, as also the similar structure of the second song, *Harmonie du soir*, with considerable subtlety and variety. Thus they have a kind of formality - the effect indeed is not dissimilar, in a looser way, to the couplet-repetitions identical in all 21 poems of *Pierrot Lunaire* - and this element of formality in the structure, compared to the rhapsody of the Wagner (which of course forms part of a much larger whole) is the appropriate result of setting a stanzaic poem. Nevertheless the Debussy is *durchkomponiert* in a way almost unique in his work; the strophic is lost in the forward flow.

Something of the same scope and density can be seen in all the other Baudelaire settings, even *Le jet d'eau* which, with its three verses each followed by a refrain, is the simplest in form and in style most premonitory of Debussy's later songs. The sense of these songs being saturated in the harmony of *Tristan* is particularly vivid in *Harmonie du soir* and the last of the set, *La mort des amants* — but, just because the saturation is so ubiquitous as well as so immediate, it is impossible to isolate any particular progression and trace it confidently to a Wagnerian source. However in the fourth song, *Recueillement*, the reference to *Tristan* is more explicit, though even here it is difficult to say just how it can be defined. Plainly it is not a direct quotation in the spirit at once inspired and pedantic of the one in the last movement of Berg's *Lyric Suite,* nor even a direct citation for obvious expressive and picturesque reasons as in Bax's *Tintagel.*

Rather it is a kind of fascinated doodling round the *Tristan*-chord as it appears in the passage where Tristan draws Isolde down onto the flowery bank at the beginning of the Act II love-duet (Ex. 15a). The opening of *Recueillement* (Ex. 15b) is ostensibly in C# minor, but in fact the chord in bar 2 has the effect of causing the C# in bars 1 and 3 to sound like a suspension over a dominant 7th of A major. The Wagner passage begins on an E pedal, building up a more chromatic form of the same suspension, then instead of going to A sideslips to D with added sixth and Lydian fourth (bar 5) and slowly descends in the next four bars, touching again in bar 8 on the same dominant 7th of A with added C#, until it rests (bar 9 into bar 10) on a chord very close to the opera's seminal chord; the one alteration necessary happens in bar 11, the D making a pure version of the *Tristan*-chord. In bars 5-6 of the Debussy the E pedal still suggests a dominant 7th of A, but the second half of each bar presents instead the diminished 7th chord C D#F#A; bar 6 decorates this chord with suspensions, bar 7 gives it plain; and with exactly the same memorable motion as Wagner uses to pass from his bar 9 to bar 10, Debussy passes to his bar 8.

This is the bar I called 'a fascinated doodle round the *Tristan*-

Ex. 15a   *Tristan*, v.s., pp. 205-6 (only harmonic movement indicated)

Ex. 15b   *Recueillement*, bars 1-8 (*Cinq Poèmes . . .*, p. 25)

Ex. 15c i   Wagner

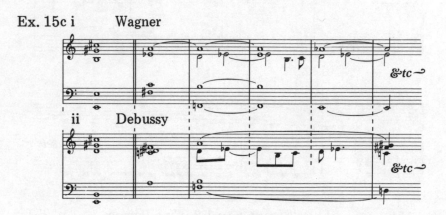

ii   Debussy

Ex. 15d   *Recueillement (Cinq Poèmes . . . , p. 26)*

chord'. Clearly this one bar of *Recueillement* does just the same as
bars 11-13 of the Wagner. Ex. 15c gives a simpler indication of the
whole process; it concludes in the *Tristan* example with six more
bars of a pedal oscillating between F♭ and E♭, eventually an
unambiguous E♭ seventh, and five bars later into an unclouded A♭

Conclusion

major. The resolution of the Debussy is quoted (Ex. 15d) – the passage ends in a C major which immediately becomes obscured with mysterious sevenths, ninths, and elevenths; and the means whereby he arrives there are an empirical alchemy unknown to Wagner.

A couple of songs in the contemporary Verlaine settings which form the *Ariettes Oubliées* (1888) – *L'ombre des arbres* and *Spleen* – show something of the same 'saturated' style, and in *Spleen* the motivic working-out is more concentrated even than anything in the Baudelaire settings; but these two songs are too short to be described as possessing Wagnerian scope. The quality of heady voluptuousness in the *Cinq Poèmes* can be followed as it is gradually muted to accommodate poems of a delicate and limpid eroticism. *En sourdine* from the first set of *Fêtes Galantes* (1892), the intense but constrained eroticism of *La Chevelure* from the *Chansons de Bilitis* of 1897 (with its climax on the *Tristan*-chord) and the last song – *Colloque sentimental* – of the second set of *Fêtes Galantes*, are the high points in this progression, which is one of increasing refinement and austerity, culminating in the clear melted snow of the Tristan l'Hermite settings of 1904-10, particularly *Auprès de cette grotte sombre* and *Je tremble en voyant ton visage*, and the mysterious simplicities of the Mallarmé settings of 1913.

3. Conclusion

The songs, therefore, form one of the paths by which Debussy became non-Wagnerian and eventually in practice anti-Wagnerian. His main non- and anti-Wagnerian development however is seen in the piano works. Debussy's piano style is for this reason outside my range, but it can briefly be formulated here, for the sake of contrast with the songs, as a growth from a nondescript *salon*-style to an original 'rediscovery of the instrument' whose mastery and brilliance is never in question even when the musical content is patently thin. The awakening of Debussy's mature piano technique does not get under way until 1903 with the *Estampes*. On the other hand the songs from the *Cinq Poèmes* onwards begin rich and complex, and are progressively sublimated into fastidious austerity.

47

It is as if the Wagnerian strain in Debussy is associated with poets — Verlaine, Baudelaire, Louÿs — whose style he outgrows, or at least loses the inclination to set to music. The energy and originality of these songs, but not the Wagnerian element, goes instead into the piano works, which had begun and continued throughout the 1880s and '90s in relative triviality, but which now take on a range and power whose ultimate achievement, in certain of the *Etudes* of 1915, is comparable in richness and complexity to the *Cinq Poèmes*. After 1892 or so the Wagnerian element goes into the stage-work, where the pressure of the Wagnerian subject-matter, that setting of individual lyrics can no longer contain, is fully able to be expressed.

La Damoiselle élue and the *Cinq Poèmes de Charles Baudelaire* show between them the several aspects of Debussy's debt to Wagner[1]. The songs in their *Tristan*-soaked style are manifestly influenced by Wagner, and it is this direct influence that in Debussy's mature music is gradually refined out of recognition. But in as much as their outward equipment — the motivic *durchkomponiert* aspect already shown — is Wagnerian, this is atypical in Debussy's mature style and represents the Wagner whom Debussy came consciously to reject. The almost Straussian (though quite un-Strauss-like) exuberance of these songs might well have indicated a different direction from the one Debussy actually took, and tendencies pulling against those for which he eventually settled. Such a Debussy would undoubtedly, on this evidence, have been a master; but one would hardly conceive him able to achieve the radically new.

And this is just what *La Damoiselle élue* does imply. It is imbued with a verdancy and consciousness of power that indicates the young Debussy's self-discovery of what he was best suited to do, both in subject-matter and in the music that embodies it. That this sureness is *Parsifal*-inspired is of the greatest importance in understanding his later development. For in style and in subject *La Damoiselle* is the first of his 'Wagnerian' works. In the course of Debussy's continuing relation to Wagner, *Tristan*, which provides the plot of *Pelléas* and touches of expressive colour everywhere, finally gives way before a *Parsifal* not softened as in *La Damoiselle*

---

1. *L'après-midi d'un faune*, another work of the same years (slightly later) and stylistic orientation, is a special case, and will be discussed in the last chapter.

48

but fully assimilated (in however wayward a fashion). *Parsifal* is the instrument of Debussy's achievement of his profoundest aims.

Note: Proses Lyriques

A piece of Wagnerian imagery is to be found in the first of the *Proses Lyriques* of 1892-3, for which Debussy wrote his own texts. This passage speaks in a 'rêve ancien' of the lost days of chivalry:

> Nul ne leur dédiera plus la fierté des casques d'or
> Maintenant ternis, à jamais ternis.
> Les chevaliers sont morts
> Sur le chemin du Grâal![1]

(pp. 5-6).

In its sense of the romance and inaccessibility of knights in armour, this is reminiscent of Parsifal's tale of his boyhood:

> And once I saw a glittering array of men on noble
> creatures pass the edge of the forest: fain had I
> been like them; with laughter they swept on their
> way. Now far I ran, yet could I not overtake them.[2]

(v.s. pp. 176-8)

— particularly if these, too, were knights of the Grail! Debussy's one-bar ostinato rhythm over a pedal-note might be called a distant reminiscence of the similar motif in Parsifal's narration (where it is a theme associated with the demonic aspect of Kundry) — but it is a marginal connection.

---

1. No one will again dedicate (to the ladies) the pride of the golden helmets, now tarnished forever. The knights on the way of the Grail are dead!
2. Margaret Glyn's translation.

CHAPTER III

THEORY OF OPERA

1. *Wagner's Theory*

Wagner's theoretical view of opera, as expressed principally in *Oper und Drama* of 1851, may be summed up for the present purpose in the following account, pieced together largely in his own words (the italics are always his). He elevated for opera an ideal of Unity: the poet alone was incomplete – he shows 'an unrealized poetic intention'; the composer alone was incomplete also – 'for although feelings may well be aroused by purely musical means, they cannot by such means be fixed as to their actual nature.' So the separation of opera into distinct poetical and musical forms was to be abandoned; also the other arts, of dance, mime, and scenic painting, even architecture, were to be amalgamated into the Unity. All would be fused together in a new equilibrium, in which, moreover, each would find a fulfilment more perfect than when left in a state of aesthetic purity.

The resulting *Gesamtkunstwerk* was to be of a completeness transcending the old stage unities of time, space and action, in a new unity of expression, an expression 'whose parts are interconnected and constantly evoke the total context.' All external influences were to be contained within the unity of expression, and 'thus the real drama. . . is something organically being and becoming, which, prompted by its own internal conditions, develops and forms itself by the one required contact with the external world, namely the necessity of making its manifestations understood'.

The unity of expression was to be accomplished by the orchestra. 'The orchestra is the agent which constantly completes the unity of expression' – it binds poetry and music and the other subsidiary arts into one dramatic whole. Though great powers were attributed to the orchestra, by its 'ability to evoke past and future in such a way that the feelings that have been aroused continue on their level of elevation', it is important to remember that it remained only 'the agent'. The orchestra was not to be indulged for its own sake, but must always be subservient to 'the poetic intention', which here (Wagner's terms tend to be fluid) can be paraphrased as 'the unified balance of all the forces making up the drama'. When the characters are in command of the art-work the orchestra remains accompanimentary; but, 'sparingly', only at 'pillars of the dramatic structure', it is allowed to come forward with its own overt expression.

The chief among several contradictions here is between the role of the music *as such* and the role of the orchestra as binding agent for the 'unity of expression'. This contradiction appears clearly in Wagner's spirited and more specific denunciation of the 'error of the art-genre of opera':-

> The dramatic aim, thus bare within and hollow, passed manifestly over into the mere intentions of the composer. . . and thus he found himself saddled with the unnatural task of. . . imagining and calling into life. . . of virtually penning the drama, of making his music not merely its expression but its *content;* and yet this content, by the very nature of things, was to be none other than the drama's self!

Music has usurped 'unnaturally' her function; the 'mere intentions of the composer' have become the *raison d'être* of the whole genre; whereas it should be subordinate, helping 'sparingly' to further the real content, the *drama,* 'the very nature of things'. These criticisms are applied even to the best examples in the unreformed operatic tradition.

This apparent conflict between 'music' and 'the orchestra' must be examined more closely. The orchestra is Wagner's vehicle for the achievement of the fusion of the arts; this orchestra was to be the symphonic orchestra, that ever-more-flexible instrument developed to its sublimest height in Beethoven's IXth Symphony and taken further still in boldness by Berlioz and Liszt. Wagner was always aware that the chief weapon for his assault and eventual conquest over the 'bare within and hollow' was such an ideal of orchestral usage.

Yet it seems as if the likelihood that this orchestra, having been assembled, should then produce *music* escapes Wagner's theoretical grasp; indeed the theoretical function of the orchestra is quite other than that of making music, for music itself is dismissed in the oddest but most unambiguous terms:

Music as an art of *expression,* can in its utmost wealth of such expression be nothing more than *true;* it has, therefore, to concern itself only with *what* it should express. . . with all its perverse efforts, music, or at least effective music, has actually remained nothing else than expression.

The impression is unavoidable that Wagner, while allotting a supreme importance to his orchestra, takes actually rather a low view of the music the orchestra must inevitably play. That 'effective music' has 'remained nothing else than expression' can only be glossed by another of Wagner's fluid reversals of the value of words — for although 'expression' has previously been given the highest place in the scale of dramatic unities, it here carries an unmistakable note of derogation. But the main oddity is the strong impression Wagner gives that, eventually, he does not value music very highly. His final castigation is of music's 'efforts to make in itself a content'; thereby, one would have thought, giving a lie to abstract symphonic music as well as to the conventionally operatic. The exact function of music as a handmaid who permits dramatic expression to be invincible, is never defined: nor is a relationship of any intimacy hinted at between the dutiful handmaid and her powerful new master, the orchestra.

These anomalies must be borne in mind while reading Wagner's emphatic summary of why opera needs reforming (his capitals):-

I declare aloud that the error in the art-genre of opera consists herein:-

THAT A MEANS OF EXPRESSION (MUSIC) HAS BEEN MADE THE END, WHILE THE END OF EXPRESSION (THE DRAMA) HAS BEEN MADE THE MEANS.

2. *Wagner's Practice*

'Nothing was really changed. . . by Wagner's demand that music should be the feminine, drama the masculine principle. The effect of his own work gives the lie to his theory, for this effect rests entirely upon the music'. The confusion I have noted between the superior role of the orchestra and the relatively menial role of music in the *Gesamtkunstwerk* is resolved by this simple statement of Einstein, who moreover adds of Wagner's writings, 'it would be the height of misapprehension to try and conceive of them as the guiding stars of his career, either from the historical or aesthetic point of view'. Even in *Das Rheingold* and parts of *Die Walküre*, where the closest approximation Wagner achieved to his announced intentions is to be found, Wagner's practice often manifests strong exception to the theory. But during the composition of *Tristan* a conscious change is seen:-

> Of this work I have taken the liberty of harbouring the loftiest expectations, which follow from my theoretical ideas. I do so not because I may have given the work its form according to my system, for in writing it I completely forgot all theory, but because I here at last, with the fullest freedom and the most complete disregard of every theoretical consideration, have conducted myself in such a manner that during the execution of my plans I perceived how widely I soared out beyond my system. . .

Incidentally ignoring the new species of tautology by which one statement is placed in opposition to another of exactly the same meaning, it is plain that this remark rings like a triumphant admission of defeat. Wagner the dramatist has been swept away by Wagner the musician. He was aware of the nature of this change; his letters during the composition of *Tristan* express his self-amazement at the way in which the overwhelming flood of musical invention breaks down all impediment, rendering all theorizing nugatory.

So the outstanding 'error of the art-genre of opera' that Wagner had set himself to correct – the subordination of the words to the music – is now endorsed, in his own admittedly 'most beautiful' work, with music more than ever before the dominant factor. It is no longer a question of the orchestra's being restricted to the function of marking the 'pillars of the dramatic structure', or even of its 'ability to evoke past and future', though both these capacities are still of great importance. The characters in the drama continue to sing their words and mime their actions; but the orchestra has become the central protagonist, expressing everything, understanding and commenting upon everything that, in the drama, remains latent. Furthermore in Act II of *Tristan* the action is suspended, is actually at the mercy of the orchestra; or rather, of the pressure upon Wagner which impels him to create music rather than drama. Further yet; the very words out of which drama is made begin to disappear; they 'melt into the music, losing their very character as intelligible language'.

So Wagner's central concern, in practice, is that the drama achieve its full expression by means of music and orchestra. In places even this already radical reversion from his theoretic relation of drama and music allows the 'handmaid' to encroach still further; and for extended areas the drama can subside and the music expand to fill the forefront of the composer's and his audience's consciousness — can become, in a word, the 'content' of the drama — the very idea he so deplored.

> The poet must take his inspiration from the musician, he must listen for the whims of music, accommodate himself to the musician's bent, choose his stuff by the latter's taste, mould his characters by the timbres expedient for the purely musical combinations. . . in short. . . he must construct his drama with a single eye to the specifically musical intentions of the composer.

Thus Wagner's scornful account of the abuses of the unreformed opera; an excellent brief description of his own maturest method.

The technical means whereby music is enabled to come to the forefront is of course the leitmotif system. Debussy's objections to the leitmotifs in the *Ring,* that they were a kind of illustrative tag or 'visiting card' for the characters or objects they embodied, are characteristically perverse. For apart from its extraordinary power to enrich the symbolic and psychological life of the drama, the leitmotif is the principal solution to the purely musical problem of sustaining compositional continuity on such an unprecedented scale. Wagner's leitmotifs are his musical material, just as Beethoven in the first movement of the IXth Symphony had his material, which they both proceed, in their respective contexts, to develop. Wagner's context is, naturally, the development of the drama, and does not follow a scheme of tonal ratiocination. Nevertheless, to re-employ his own words, he has constructed his drama 'with a single eye to the specifically musical intentions of the composer', and although in his case dramatist and composer are one and the same, the 'mere intentions of the composer' are those of the dramatist too.

3. Debussy's Practice and Lack of Theory

'Is it like this all the time?' 'Yes'. 'Nothing more? There's nothing in it. No music. It has nothing consecutive. No musical phrases. No development. . . I am first and foremost a musician. If there is music in a work I want it to dominate, it must not be subordinate to any other claim. . . There's not enough music in this work. Delicate harmonies, excellent orchestral effects, in very good taste. But it amounts to nothing, nothing at all. *You might as well be listening to the play of Maeterlinck as it was, without the music.*'

Thus Richard Strauss during his visit to *Pelléas* with Romain Rolland in 1907. Not perhaps the best guide to Debussy, Strauss has nevertheless in his forthright fashion touched upon the crux of the relationship of Debussy to Wagner as a composer of opera. A similar view to that of Strauss was given by Ernest Newman, in language still more straightforward.

'For my own part . . . . I have never been able to see *(Pelléas)*, so far as regards its form, as anything but an expression of artistic bankruptcy'; and again, 'Wagner had in him by instinct what Debussy never had — the desire for flawless logic in music . . . Debussy and his fellows have laboured under the delusion that form could be replaced by style . . .'

This bad old view originates in *Pelléas's* earliest reception, as the following mélange of journalistic reaction to the première in 1902 makes clear:-

' — Neither melody, rhythm, leitmotif, nor charm. . .' 'music which is not music. . . not even declamation. . .' 'of melody there is not the slightest pretention. . . the same results would be obtained if the singers were to declaim their parts instead of singing them. . .' 'Debussy has arrived at the greatest negation of every doctrine. . . disowns melody. . . despises the symphony with all its resources. . .' 'Claude Debussy, the greatest of living De-composers'.

This view at its least sympathetic says, like Strauss, that *Pelléas* is simply *ohne Musik*. Put by a critic sympathetic to Debussy, it can say (as does Grout in *A Short History of Opera*) that 'the final score cannot be said to owe anything to Wagner beyond the orchestral continuity, the use of leitmotifs, and the exclusion of all merely ornamental details'. Even Joseph Kerman in *Opera as Drama* can still say that 'Wagner and Debussy. . . stand at opposite poles of the celebrated nineteenth-century operatic 'reform'.' Something in Debussy's opera inspires this many-levelled unanimity of assurance that he and Wagner are antithetical. The differences are true enough (and Professor Kerman gives a most sensitive account of them); but the connections are at least as important, and much more interesting.

Debussy had no theory of opera (his stance is to be instinctive and anti-theoretical in all artistic matters); his rationale has to be deduced from his operatic practice, and from such random reflections on the subject as can be gleaned from the pages of *M. Croche* and Vallas. [1] The impression from the literary sources is only partially suggestive. Vallas has a paragraph about Debussy's disdain for opera as a genre — he speaks of his 'dislike for dramatic works', and the faults 'which made the writing of a good opera an utter impossibility'.

But this is too elementary; Vallas elsewhere gives an interesting passage on Wagner which is worth reproducing at length. 'Wagner', Debussy complains,

> has accustomed us to make the music servilely dependent on the characters. I shall try to make myself clear regarding this matter, in my opinion the chief cause of the confusion which exists in the dramatic music of our times: Music has a rhythm whose secret force directs the development. The emotions of the soul have another, which is more instructively general and is influenced by numerous events. The juxtaposition of these two rhythms creates perpetual conflict. They are not simultaneous. Either the music gets out of breath in running after a character, or else the character sits down on a note to allow the music to catch up with him.

So 'a good opera', one that Debussy would not 'dislike', can come into being when the tempo of the emotions and the tempo of the music are synchronized. 'Amazing encounters between these two forces often take place', Debussy continues, 'and Wagner can claim the honour of having provoked some of them.' Debussy then proceeds sharply to attack 'the application of the symphonic form to dramatic action', since Wagner's successes are merely 'due to chance' (this, in the context of the rest of the passage, is disappointingly lacking in penetration; for the truth is surely the reverse).

1. Vallas: *The Theories of Claude Debussy.*

Debussy does provide another interesting remark about opera, in his 'statement. . . to the Opéra-Comique on the occasion of a revival' of *Pelléas*. Here he defends his prosody, which was (as their reactions have shown) much misunderstood by critics of the first production. 'The characters of this drama' (he writes)

> endeavour to sing like real persons and not in an arbitrary language built on antiquated traditions. Hence the reproach levelled at my alleged partiality for monotone declamation, in which there is no trace of melody.

('Like real persons' must be understood figuratively of course — Debussy means a naturalistic convention of word-setting as opposed to an artificial convention). His utterances, taken together, suggest that an opera's musical prosody must be natural, not rhetorical; and that its musical pace should be sensitively attuned to the pace of its expression of its emotions; these points both necessitate abandoning the symphonic aspect. By itself this is not much more than a starting-point for a theory of opera.

But taken with Debussy's operatic *practice* such an idea of his theory is much extended, though certainly along similar lines. In *Pelléas* 'the poet alone is incomplete. . . the composer alone is incomplete also'; 'the orchestra is the agent which constantly completes the unity of expression' through its 'ability to evoke past and future', though it 'must not be indulged for its own sake, but must always be subservient to "the poetic intention" '; the orchestra however must remain accompanimentary, but 'sparingly', only at 'pillars of the dramatic structure', it is allowed to come forward into overt expression: in short, music is to be the 'handmaid' of the dramatic expression, so that the great 'error in the art-genre' of most opera up to and emphatically including Wagner — that 'the means of expression (music) has been made the end, while the end of expression (the drama) has been made the means' — may be rectified. Such is Debussy's practice, in *Pelléas*, and as these reminders[1] from my account of Wagner's theory show, it concurs precisely with Wagner's intentions as expressed in *Oper und Drama*, but ignored in his mature practice.

1. All from pp. 50-52 above.

4. Conclusion

It is hardly original to point out that Debussy's *Pelléas* fulfils better than any of Wagner's works the theoretical demands of *Oper und Drama;* but the positions nonetheless are far from clear. On the one hand there are as it were 'Wagnerian' critics, who argue, from Debussy's antagonism to Wagner, and above all from the obvious differences in their cultural and musical ethos, that Debussy represents the focal point of reaction against Wagner, or as Kerman says, that they are 'opposite poles' of the same movement. On the other we have those who see clearly how Debussy realizes in all its pureness what in Wagner had been only an idea, yet still either insist that his differences — his enthusiasm for Mussorgsky, his dislike of formulae, his place in a long though much-interrupted heritage of fastidious clarity in the matter of operatic declamation[1], in a word, his Frenchness — somehow make his opera unWagnerian. If these critics acknowledge Wagner, they somehow fail to take the consequences.

The truth (though Debussy would not have enjoyed it) is that *Pelléas* is Wagnerian both in theory and in practice; but it does not correspond to Wagner's practice because this has at best only an equivocal relation to his theory, and more typically is its thorough negation. Clearly the immediate risk in Debussy's practice, to use again his own words, is that 'the music gets out of breath[2] in running after a character', and the complementary risk in Wagner's practice, that 'the character sits down on a note to allow the music to catch up with him'. Nonetheless the greater danger for Debussy lies in the thinness of substance that could result from so thoroughgoing an endorsement of a theory whose fulfillment denies the domination of music. When Auden called *Pelléas* 'one of the great anti-operas' he paid tribute to a success achieved against the nature of the genre, which indeed to a certain extent denies the genre's *raison d'être*. These matters will be taken up in the chapters following, devoted to various aspects of Debussy's opera *sub specie*

---

1. Cf. Rolland's famous account of the first night of *Pelléas*. He calls it ' a very notable event in the history of French music ', and evokes as touchstones the premières of Lully's *Cadmus et Hermione*, Rameau's *Hippolyte et Aricie*, and Gluck's *Iphigénie en Aulide*.

2. Cf. ' . . . the inability of the thought or the emotion [of Debussy] to get into a *decently long stride*. ' Newman again; my italics.

Wagner. First the connections of plot that make *Pelléas* a virtual
impression from *Tristan;* then the exploration of Wagnerian
recollections and assimilations in the music. *Prima le verbe, doppo
la musica* — but even in the prosody-opera, the music, in the end,
is victor.

CHAPTER IV

PELLEAS AND TRISTAN

1. *Plot and Subject-Matter*

Elliot Zuckerman in his book on *The First Hundred Years of Wagner's Tristan* remarks that 'the plot of *Tristan* could have been the model for Maeterlinck's tenuous account of an inexplicably fated love'. The outer events of *Tristan und Isolde* and *Pelléas et Mélisande* are far from dissimilar — or, to put it differently, the two love-affairs whose progress they relate would appear much of a muchness in a divorce-court. The sensitive observer, however, could not but concentrate upon the atmospheric differences, and these might well, in the end, prove decisive.

The outer events are as follows. Queen Isolde (who already nourishes a powerful desire for her elderly consort's young hero-nephew), heedless of her shrewd maid-servant's warnings, seizes the first opportunity after her marriage to consummate her desires. She and her lover spend the night together in the garden; but unfortunately a trusty servant of the King has noticed what is amiss, and arranges an elaborate trick whereby the pair may be taken in mid-guilt. The nephew, conscious as he must be of his indefensible position, offers no resistance in the ensuing sword-fight; he soon after dies of his wounds, whereupon his lady, who has fled away to join him, succumbs to her overwhelming grief.

And of the other version; an ageing man of unpredictably violent disposition discovers an unknown girl lost in a wood. They marry, but are not complementary; she flirts with his half-brother, a younger man, who manifests the ardour and tenderness her husband lacks. He, all-trusting, seems at first positively to throw the lovers together, but in the end an ever-increasing violence of jealousy causes him to spy on them as they meet in the garden at night, and himself to kill the young man, only to be overcome with remorse as his wife, weakened by his cruel insistence as well as by child-birth, dies too.

These are the outward actions, the 'divorce-court' version of the events, in which the second evidently follows the first quite closely. But it is now necessary to distinguish sharply between Plot, meaning the outward paraphernalia of events, and Subject – the interior exposition of the heart of the matter. I have outlined the mere plot, in its *Tristan* and its *Pelléas* version; but the differences of emphasis in the two works render this similarity surprisingly unobtrusive. For the subject of *Tristan und Isolde* is Passion, or rather, as Mann put it, 'sensuality, enormous sensuality. . . sensuality unquenchable by any amount of gratification'. Whereas the subject of *Pelléas et Mélisande* is loneliness, lack of connection – in the end a frigid nihilism. This fundamental difference in the two treatments of virtually the same plot, must always be borne in mind during the following account of the correspondences between the two works.

2. *The outside world*

Both operas subsist in a kind of social void. Constant Lambert once remarked that comparison of the off-stage sailors' choruses in the first acts of *Tristan* and *Pelléas* provided a microcosm of their respective composer's mannerisms. In the former they sing vigorous anti-Irish songs in a four-square *Meistersinger*-Guild style, in the latter they are restricted to mysterious cries of 'hisse-hoé, hisse-hoé.' These choruses could also stand for the way in which, in both operas, the world at large remains as it were off-stage. This is exceptional in Wagner, all of whose other operas concern themselves with a wide range of relationships, whether social, familial, psychological, or ritualized.

But in *Tristan* the external world essentially does not count; in Act I the sailors and, at the end, the jubilant crowd, form a hallucinatory backcloth to the protagonists' discovery of their passion; at the beginning of Act II courtly society rides away into the night, the hunting-horns become more and more magically distant, the lovers are left alone to their rapt self-absorption; and every listener has shared their impatience that the external world simply recede. Even the interruption of the lovers is private, not at all a public exposure; its privacy gives the opportunity, the pretext almost, for

Marke's *scena* and the strophic song that delivers the lovers more firmly than before into the arms of each other and of death, while the reappearance of the unfriendly world in the arrival of the second ship towards the end of Act III, and the consequent confusion and fighting, always seems something of a blemish in an action that, without them, might be understood as completely internalized.

Isolde and Tristan absorb each other absolutely throughout Act II — the absorption is marvellously rendered by their bemused reaction to the expectant crowd as the ship pulls in at the end of Act I) '... wer naht? ... welcher Konig?' ... 'wo bin ich?'[1]; then in the first part of Act III Tristan totally absorbs himself, and finally Isolde is ravished away in self-absorption. The opera's subject, passion, ('des welterwerden's Walterin' — Venus, the universal law-giver) demands this complete subjection to its sway.

In *Pelléas* the action suspires in a vacuum more thorough-going still. Mélisande arrives from nowhere, Pelléas wishes to set off on an unspecified journey; symbols of futility and helplessness abound in the text as in the action, principal among them the aura of gloomy inexplicability surrounding the existence of the sick King. There are sailors who sing 'hisse-hoé', and chambermaids who fall to their knees as Mélisande dies. There are paupers revealed by the sudden surprise of moonlight as Pelléas and Mélisande look for the lost ring in the cave by the sea, and Pelléas's frightened muttering tells of a famine in Allemonde. Such isolation of the characters from any social context is of course deliberate on Maeterlinck's part; the symbols of the mysterious ship, the impenetrable forest, the blind man's well, and so forth, are effective if slightly common-place adjuncts to a portrayal of human isolation.

The social vacuum here is not, as in *Tristan,* designed to throw the intimacy and passion of the lovers into heightened relief. It extends beyond the background of the characters; it comes forward and envelops them. The lovers and the wronged husband do not stand out as protagonists; they merge, with the old King, the Queen, the child, into the background; they are made, as indeed all the characters are, to become as symbolic as the gloomy castle, the escaped doves, or the stench of death in the vaults beneath the castle. They stand for something; they are not themselves. The opera's subject, human isolation ('c'était un pauvre petit être mystérieux comme tout le monde' — she was a sad mysterious

1. Tristan: ' Who comes? ... what king? ' Isolde: ' Where am I? ' (v.s. pp. 125-6).

little being — 'poor all of us, when you come to think of it') demands this listless denial of straightforward humanity.

3. *Marke and Melot—Golaud and Arkel*

The attributes of old King Marke, the wronged but forgiving husband in *Tristan,* are in *Pelléas* shared between the ancient King Arkel, and his grandson, the not-youthful Golaud. Arkel corresponds to Marke's aspect as a commentator, whose action in the plot is small but whose presence is great. They stand aloof, and from their wise isolation understand, pity, and forgive. They both submit to grief, and as commentators have sometimes to utter the words that everyone on stage and in the audience must feel. Marke does so in a noble outburst. . . 'Tod denn Alles! Alles tot!'[1] and sobs; Arkel constrains his grief — 'Mais la tristesse, Golaud . . . mais la tristesse de tout ce que l'on voit . . .'[2]

Golaud takes over the other aspect of Marke, that of the wronged elderly husband whose marriage, in *Tristan* a piece of political strategy, in *Pelléas* simply fortuitous, is betrayed by a faithless young wife. Golaud has all of Marke's anguish, which turns not into noble abnegation but to jealousy, spying, and eventual murder of the rival— in *Tristan* his nephew, in *Pelléas* his halfbrother.

Melot too has a place in this equation, Tristan's treacherous friend who organizes the night-hunt ostensibly to enable the lovers to enjoy their secret meeting, but in fact to stage a sensational discovery of their adultery. Melot's motive is jealousy of Tristan, a mingling of jealousy for Tristan's warm place in the King's affection, and for his conquest of Isolde.[3] And it is Melot who in fact gives Tristan the sword wound which is the physical reason for his death.

Golaud then is a merging of the role of Marke as a wronged husband with a much extended aspect of Melot as a jealous and mur-

1. ' Dead then all! All dead. ' (*Tristan* v.s. p. 374).

2. ' But the sadness, Golaud . . . but the sadness of everything one sees . . . ' (*Pelléas* v.s. pp. 305-6).

3. The first is Brangäne's view—' From Tristan to Marke is Melot's way, and there he sows evil seed. ' (v.s. pp. 144-5); Tristan's (v.s. p. 270) inclines to the second—' Your glance, Isolde, dazzled him too; my friend betrayed me through envious passion. '

derous friend. Arkel, who at the end of *Pelléas* says 'C'est terrible mais ce n'est pas vôtre faute . . .'[1] takes over the conciliatory aspect of Marke, the King who has sped over the seas to forgive, pleading 'wie selig, das den Freund ich frei von Schuld da fand!'[2]

4. *The Lovers*

There is contrast rather than resemblance in the characterization of the lovers. Throughout Act I Tristan and Isolde burn with mutual awareness, transparently veiled on her part by proud anger, and on his by courtly but weary resentment. The memory of the recent events in Ireland rankles, and the future holds no prospect of pleasure. The love-potion tears aside the veil; inhibition at once surrenders to the 'wilds of passion', the 'unquenchable sensuality' that Nietzsche did not dare name.[3] Whereas the best characterization of the love of Pelléas and Mélisande is given by Golaud in Act V:- 'Ils s'étaient embrassés comme des petits enfants. . . Ils étaient frère et soeur.'[4] Their love consists of a certain pleasure in each other's company, from which Golaud feels excluded; a delicate flirtatiousness on the part of Mélisande, on that of Pelléas a timid tenderness. Hardly have they been able to whisper 'Je t'aime' . . . 'je t'aime aussi', before Golaud is upon them with an avenging sword.

So it is in the treatment of the central core of the drama — the lovers — that the intentions of Debussy and Wagner are most antipathetic. This has frequently been pointed out, but always interpreted as a *reaction*, thus: Debussy is satiated by (and anyway, incapable of) the Wagnerian surge of ardour and passion, so therefore takes his love-scene to the opposite extreme; he has his lovers whisper their avowals with the orchestra completely silent.

I think that it is mistaken to interpret the difference of treatment in this way, as a reaction or even revulsion on Debussy's

1. ' It is dreadful, but it is not your fault. ' (v.s. p. 308).
2. ' What joy that I find my Tristan free of blame. ' (v.s. p. 378).
3. ' Who will dare to utter the word, the right word, for the *ardeurs* of the *Tristan*-music? '
4. ' They embraced like little children . . . they were brother and sister. '

part. The treatment of the two pairs of lovers, and in particular of the two love-scenes (*Tristan* II ii and *Pelléas* IV iv) is the clearest indication of Wagner's and Debussy's different *subject* even when dealing with the same *plot*. To recapitulate and extend the area of the contrast: Wagner's subject-matter is human fulfilment-in-love and fulfilment of love-in-death, his means of expression the full musical resources of German orchestral-symphonic composition; Debussy's subject-matter is human loneliness and sadness, and his means of expression an extension of the strictest observation of French prosody into the domain of the musical theatre.

Wagner in *Tristan* was expressing himself; he and Mathilde Wesendonk furnish the fuel for the subject-matter of passion. His letters to her make great play with the direct transfusion of life into art and art into life; and in more general terms he said that he wished his opera to be a monument to the sovereign human power of Love, whose fulfilment had been so lacking in his own life. Debussy, early on in the composition of his love-scene, wrote in a letter to Chausson 'Je me suis efforcé d'être aussi Pelléas que Mélisande'. I endeavour to be myself both Pelléas and Mélisande – the attempt to abnegate all expression of the self so characteristic of the mature Debussy, is implicit in this sentence.[1] Wagner renders life and love directly into art; Debussy illustrates with restraint, building slowly and uncertainly a work with nothing in it of auto-biographical self-expression.

It is worthwhile to go with greater detail into the working and motivation of Debussy's lovers as they derive from Wagner's. In externals the two love-scenes are remarkably similar. A hurried appointment has been made, arranging the time and place for the meeting. We wait in a mounting frenzy of impatience with Isolde for her lover; we pace anxiously up and down with Pelléas as he wonders why Mélisande is so delayed – 'Il est tard, elle ne vient pas . . .'[2]

The respective lovers now at last appear, and both pairs proceed to an expression of thankfulness and joy at each other's faithfulness; or rather in Wagner we have an ecstatic and entirely mutual

---

1. This same letter (of 1893) has spoken previously of Debussy's destruction of an earlier draft of the scene because 'the ghost of old Klingsor, alias Richard Wagner, appeared at the turning of one of the bars . . .'

2. ' It's late; she doesn't come . . . ' (v.s. pp. 233-4).

transport[1], but in Debussy only a one-(Pelléas)-sided gratitude[2] that remains more than a little tentative until he snatches a brusque kiss. Mélisande's non-participation, or at least reluctance, is important enough to be dealt with separately. Enough here to emphasize the similarity between Tristan's and Pelléas's eagerness, and the contrast between Isolde's impatience and Mélisande's reluctance to commit herself, epitomized by Wagner's *Stürmische Umarmungen Beider* and Pelléas's *brusque embrace*, as if of a passive object.

Now the two lovers indulge in breathless explanation and reminiscence of the events that have kept them apart. Tristan and Isolde relive the tensions of Act I and the events in Ireland previous to the action of the opera. The nightmare of separation amidst an alien world is over; it is vital to them to pour out to each other their confused impressions of the dawning of love, and of the checks and prohibitions they have had to undergo, before the music quietens and relaxes, and the love duet proper begins. It is noticeable in this section that Isolde's music, though she participates as vigorously as her lover, always shows a tendency towards melodic and harmonic relaxation, anticipating the central slow section, whereas Tristan's rejoinders spur the music back into excited momentum. Mélisande's explanation of her lateness preserves anxiety at the expense of ardour — 'vôtre frère avait un mauvais rêve. Et puis ma robe s'est accrochée au clou de la porte.'[3]

Pelléas, moodily impatient before Mélisande's arrival, had sung 'Il faut que je lui dise tout ce que je n'ai pas dit . . .'[4], his inability 'to dare to utter the word for his *ardeurs*' is perhaps in strongest contrast to Wagner's torrent of expression. The 'word' in Wagner — 'O Wonne der Seele, o süsse, hehrste, kühnste, schönste, seligste

---

1. v.s. pp. 164 f.
2. v.s. pp. 242 f.
   P. This is perhaps the last time I'll see you . . . I must go away for ever.
   M. Why do you always say you're going away?
   P. I must tell you what you know already! Don't you know what I'm going to tell you?
   M. But no, no, I know nothing.
   P. You don't know why I have to take myself off . . . you don't know that it's because . . . [he kisses her abruptly] . . . I love you.
3. ' Your brother had a bad dream. And then my dress got caught on a nail in the gate. ' (v.s. pp. 238-9).
4. ' I must tell her everything I've not said . . . ' (v.s. p. 236).

Lust! Überreiche! überschwänglich! hocherhab'ne! Freudejauchz-
en! Lustentzucken! Himmel-' (to a tremendous soprano top C) –
'höchstes Weltentrücken!'[1] – is uttered again and again: the constraint of Debussy's two timid lovers is best shown in Pelléas's mur-
mured 'on a brisé la glace' (più pp) 'avec des fers rougis!'[2]

5. The love-duets

The preliminaries over, the love-duets proper begin respectively
at 'O sink' hernieder'[3] and 'On dirait que ta voix a passé sur la mer
au printemps'.[4] In the simple mechanics of the action the men take
the lead – Pelléas had asked Mélisande to come from the moonlight into the shadows, she was reluctant and he insisted.[5] Later
he wishes her to come out again into the light, though this time
her refusal is accepted.[6] Tristan 'draws Isolde gently down towards
him onto a flowery bank'.[7] But this male initiative in stage-mani-
pulation is matched by the more important male dominance in the
music. Tristan begins every phrase of 'O sink' hernieder', which is
at once echoed by Isolde[8]; until the voices join together as 'the
world fades away'.[9] The next extension of the theme is initiated
by Isolde and taken up by Tristan,[10] during which she gives the
first intimation of the full love-theme, which he imitates, then
again the voices join – 'selbst dann bin ich die Welt' – in a mutual
celebration of 'Liebe heiligstes Leben . . .'[11] The end of this first
stage of the duet is marked by Brangäne's first interlude. Then the
duet continues with more sustained exchanges between the two
lovers[12] and Tristan 'gently draws Isolde to him' and gives out the
first leading statement of the *Liebestod* theme.[13] It is like a lesson;

1. ' O joy of the soul, O sweetest, highest, boldest, loveliest, holiest joy! . . . too rich!
too blessed! . . . exuberance of rapture! joyous shouting! vaulting rapture! Highest
heavens' world-forgetting! '
2. ' We have broken the ice with red-hot irons '. (v.s. p. 244).
3. v.s. p. 206.
4. v.s. p. 245.
5. v.s. pp. 236-7.
6. v.s. pp. 252-3.
7. v.s. p. 205.
8. v.s. pp. 206-8.
9. v.s. pp. 209-10.
10. v.s. pp. 210-11.
11. v.s. pp. 212-4.
12. v.s. pp. 219-26.
13. v.s. pp. 226-9.

she 'looking to him in rapt contemplation' repeats after him every phrase, their voices gradually coalesce, and Brangäne's second distant warning delineates the close of the second stage of the duet. The third begins[1] with further exchange, in which the exaltation and excitement of the opening of the act gradually return; the voices rise in increasing rapture, and take up[5] and expand the *Liebestod* theme in ever-extending sequences until interrupted by the shriek from Brangäne and the precipate entry of Kurwenal, then Marke, Melot and the courtiers. All these changes of section are clearly marked by perfect cadences which stand out with great prominence and beauty in the context of chromatic restlessness; at the interruption of the lovers the tonality too is drastically interrupted.

So in the *Tristan* duet passion is expressed with unwithholding mutuality, on the whole with the man taking the initiatory role and the woman eagerly responding. It consists of a musical exposition and development of some length; and, in spite of its appearance of effortless flow, is clearly divided into three sections separated by the two interpolations of Brangäne, who is invisible and, since her words are so spaced out, virtually speechless too.

Debussy's love-scene is of course not conceived on this enormous scale. Nevertheless there are some important points of contact though not of similarity. It is Pelléas who, like Tristan, initiates, questions, who is eager and fervent; but Mélisande does not respond.

The contrast between the scope and symphonic élan of the Wagner love-scene in which however the lovers never even say they love each other, and the silence of the orchestra into which Debussy's lovers whisper 'Je t'aime'. . . 'je t'aime aussi. . .' has often been remarked; also that the only other embrace between Pelléas and Mélisande is accompanied by a brief bar of silence. All this would seem to indicate Debussy's characteristically different (more refined, less sustained) approach from Wagner's in dealing with the same plot-situation. But the plot-situation is not the same — the role of Pelléas corresponds to that of Tristan, but the love-scene in *Pelléas* is almost a monologue from him, and such exchanges as the lovers make tend to show rather their separateness than their mutuality.

1. v.s. p. 230.
2. v.s. p. 238 f.

Mélisande seems never to return feeling — to Pelléas alone belongs all the rapture, and his rapture hardly for a moment loses the anxiety that had characterized his utterance before her arrival. 'Mais pourquoi m'aimes-tu?. . . est-ce vrai, ce que tu dis?. . . Tu ne mens pas un peu, pour me faire sourire?. . .'[1] No, she never lies, she replies, except to her husband. Pelléas's single rapture recommences[2] — 'I never saw anyone so beautiful before you. . . I searched everywhere but I never found beauty, and now' (the climax of his 'monologue') 'I have found you. . . I have found it in you. . . I believe there is no woman in the world more lovely than you!' — and immediately from this height of solitary ecstasy he asks 'Where are you? I can't hear you breathe.' And thus the conversation continues after Mélisande's refusal[3] to let Pelléas bring her out into the moonlight:—

P.   Tu ne songe pas à moi en ce moment. . .
M.   Mais si, je ne songe qu'à toi. . .
P.   Tu regardais ailleurs. . .
M.   Je te voyais ailleurs. . .
P.   Tu es distraite. . . Qu'as-tu donc? Tu ne me sembles pas heureuse. . .
M.   Si, si je suis heureuse, mais je suis triste . . .[4]

And at this ambiguous moment they hear the castle gate close behind them — their doom is soon to be sealed.

Surely it is clear that Debussy's subject even in his love-scene is not the coming-together of two lovers burning with one flame, but a further and still more protracted demonstration of their essential separateness? Mélisande is simply not in contact with Pelléas any more than she is in contact with anyone else; and it is this radical divergence from the lovers' mutuality in *Tristan* which makes *Pelléas* seem to be a reaction or revulsion against Wagner. When one sees the depth of the divergence that different subject-matters

---

1. ' But why do you love me? . . . is it true what you say? . . . you're not lying a bit, to make me smile? ' (v.s. pp. 246-7).

2. pp. 248-51.

3. v.s. p. 253.

4. P. You're not thinking of me even now . . .
    M. But I have no other thought than you . . .
    P. You were looking elsewhere . . .
    M. I saw you somewhere else . . .
    P. You are absent . . . why? . . . you don't seem happy . . .
    M. Yes, yes, I am happy . . . but I am sad . . . (v.s. pp. 254-5).

make from the same plot — in Wagner typically fulfilling, religiously and musically satisfying; in Debussy typically abnegatory, un-
satisfied and etiolated — one can also begin to get a firm hold on
the similarities, on just to what an extent the latter grew out of the
former.

6. *Mélisande and Brangäne*

I said earlier that though Golaud in the plot of *Pelléas* corresponds to Marke he contains also an admixture of Melot. The correspondence of Mélisande and Isolde as female protagonists contains
a similar superimposition. Mélisande is a palimpsest of the imper-
ious queen and her cringing confidante.

Brangäne's function in the love-duet of *Tristan* is threefold.
Before Tristan's arrival she warns Isolde of the perfidy of Melot,[1]
and she *knows* the night-hunt has been arranged as a trap.[2] Her
clarity is summed up in the line 'Weil du erblindet wähnst du den
Blick der Welt erblödet für euch?'[3] — 'because you are blinded do
you reckon the whole world is blind to you?' — but Isolde waves
aside her inferior's superior knowledge with indignant scorn. So
Brangäne knows that the interruption is bound to happen; even
simple precaution says that the lovers are doomed.

Her second function is simply for her to be present throughout
the love-scene. She keeps guard, though she knows just what form
the danger will take, and she gives the appropriate shriek when it
arrives. Her third function is more completely musical, though by
musical means it focuses attention always onto the subject of passion. Her lonely voice, singing in long notes dimly perceived
through a richly interweaving orchestral texture, of the danger inherent in the fullness of the love we and she witness on the stage,
acts as a formal device twice punctuating the three stages of the
love-duet. 'Neid'sche Wache!' — 'Envious watcher!' — Isolde calls
her. Her isolation enhances the lovers' oneness.

1. ' With ill-intentioned craft and spying glance he sought in [Tristan's] demeanour to
find there what might serve him. I've often seen him treacherously listening, how he
can secretly snare you. ' (v.s. pp. 142-3).

2. ' And so today in Council is ordered this over-hasty night-hunt; for a nobler game than
you imagine, have they set the huntsmen's trap '.

3. v.s. p. 141.

How can one say that Mélisande corresponds to this narcissistic figure? To begin with, in just this quality of narcissism. Even throughout the crucial love-scene, Mélisande is self-absorbed, almost uninterested in Pelléas — 'tu ne songes pas à moi en ce moment' as he says. Mélisande is flirtatious and cold, a fascinator, who shies away from the consequences of the emotions she arouses. All the men in the opera, even the ancient King and the young prince, feel the fascination — for Arkel it is her vulnerability, for Yniold her attraction as 'petit-mère' — but most of all, naturally, she fascinates her husband and her lover. She defies possession even while exerting the strongest attraction to be possessed. Proust has written about such people with such understanding that he might seem to be a more articulate Pelléas trying to communicate the indefinable strength of her involuntary powers:-

'. . . Even when you hold them in your hands, these people are fugitive. . .' '. . . Anxiety is born again and love. . . it is such people more than any others who inspire love in us, for our destruction.'. . . 'this sort of anxiety has a great affinity for bodies. It adds to them a quality which surpasses beauty even. . . to these people, these fugitives, their own nature, our anxiety fastens wings. . .' '. . . one of those girls beneath whose envelope of flesh . . . hidden persons are stirring . . . [and] not only these persons, but the desire, the voluptuous memory, the desperate quest of all these persons. . .'

What suits best the coquettish quality of her fascination is the scene where, leaning out of her window towards Pelléas, Mélisande's hair falls down in a Pre-Raphaelite shower around him. With him on the ground, literally at arm's length, and she safely separate in her room, a scene of voluptuous intensity develops, which has more feeling on her side, and possibly on his, than in the love-duet proper in Act IV. This scene however is still flirtatious; and moreover Golaud interrupts and furiously sends Pelléas off — from this moment his jealousy is conscious and deliberate. This scene in its relation to the love-duet proper is as a successful dress-rehearsal to a disastrous first-night.

7. *The Interruption*

Throughout Pelléas's devotions Mélisande is, in the Proustian sense, 'fugitive' — in fact in saying 'tu regardais ailleurs' Pelléas means just this, though he misinterprets and she, partly by her insistence upon remaining in the dark, covers it up. The musical function of Brangäne's interpolations have no reflection in Debussy's love-scene — it is too short-breathed, and (evidently) not enough of a real love-scene, to need such formal delineation; but the strongest parallel between her role in *Tristan* Act II and Mélisande's in *Pelléas* Act IV iv, is that Mélisande is also aware of the likelihood of interruption. Wagner's love-duet is interrupted just as the music is reaching its long-prepared climax, hence the overwhelming quality of one's disappointment at this moment. The interruption moreover is over almost immediately, cut off with a great surge of the hunting-horns that were last heard fading into the distance seemingly hours since. In Pelléas the interruption comes about half-way through the scene, at the moment reached earlier in discussing Mélisande's indifference to Pelléas's ardour. The castle gates are closed and locked, and from this point until the end the scene takes place in a state of suspension. This appears to set off in Mélisande too the chastely erotic excitement that only Pelléas has shown so far. The excitement caused in the lovers by being locked out, and then by the presence of Golaud, corresponds to Tristan and Isolde's enthusiastic adoption of the new *Liebestod* theme; in the Debussy an excitement stimulated by an external source, in the Wagner, love being nourished and sustained out of its own substance.

As Golaud's motif sounds out in varying guises Mélisande is stirred into life; to Pelléas's 'it is too late!' she cries 'Tant mieux! Tant mieux!' and he immediately is surprised by her new warmth — 'Tu?' — as if such ardour from her were never to be expected.[1] In a *Tristan*esque paradox he cries 'All is lost, all is saved!' They embrace, and Pelléas at least experiences twelve bars of ecstasy.[2] But Mélisande, in her Brangäne-aspect, is all ears — 'There's someone behind us...', though Pelléas only has ears for her heart in the darkness, and attempts to prolong the one-sided rapture. She sees

1. v.s. pp. 256-7 (Mélisande's ' tant mieux! ' is Englished as ' Thank God! ')
2. v.s. p. 258.

Golaud, he does not. She refuses to run away, and as the violent husband advances sword in hand, 'they embrace desperately'. The only spontaneous passion in the whole scene is produced by sheer fright – they are like terrified children clinging together; for two bars they sing simultaneously, he 'donne! donne!' she 'toute! toute!', Golaud strikes Pelléas down, and Mélisande flies off to the woods in terror. The dignity of Tristan and Isolde's indignity is completely lacking – Golaud would no more give utterance to Marke's lamentation than Mélisande would take up her lover's part in a stanzaic song about following him to the land of death – the act ends precipitately (even grotesquely), with an explosive violence unusual in Debussy.

Pelléas and Tristan, the lovers, both in the end fail to defend themselves against the swords of their rivals; Tristan with self-sacrificial courage, Pelléas ignominiously. Mélisande in this crucial scene corresponds with Isolde only as the requirement of the plot, as belovéd and possible adulteress; for in all other respects it is the narcissistic Brangäne-aspect that controls her behaviour. She is as remote from Pelléas's emotion almost as absolutely as if she were, like Brangäne, off-stage. But Mélisande is a Brangäne too wayward and self-absorbed even to be able to heed her own cry of warning. Brangäne and the Brangäne-aspect of Mélisande both subconsciously wish the interruption to happen (as they both know it will); Brangäne out of her lonely envy for her mistress, Mélisande gratifying a fugitive prompting towards self-destruction in the destruction of others.

8. Conclusion

Such an establishing of correspondences between the plot and the characters of *Tristan* and *Pelléas* shows Debussy to have taken up aspects that in Wagner's more comprehensive work are peripheral to the main subject of passion – the patriarchal figure of Marke with his heart-broken dignity, the jealous violence of Melot, the lonely narcissism of Brangäne—and to have made them the centre of his interests; the plot, however, remaining essentially the same.[1]

But of course Debussy is not the author of the plot of *Pelléas*!

Nevertheless I think that this does not materially affect the establishment of correspondences. There is a sense in which Wagner, also, is not strictly speaking the author of the *Tristan* story; he has drawn upon the romances, as Debussy upon Maeterlinck, to fashion from them his own interpretation and significance. Maeterlinck, moreover, is himself part of a movement whose orientation is already Wagner-inspired. And above all there is Debussy's clairvoyant identification with the play, making the claim that he might almost have written it himself as plausible (though factually preposterous) as the claim that Maeterlinck might have written it especially for Debussy. Kerman in *Opera as Drama* is particularly good on this 'most extraordinary' of 'all the ingenious, fortunate, magic convergences in the history of opera'. What I have done throughout this chapter, though it might have involved some special pleading, is to have relied implicitly upon Professor Kerman's maxim, 'In opera the composer is the dramatist'.

But wherein does the *musical* resemblance lie? Between the full-blooded chromatic orchestral overflow of *Tristan* and the pentatonic, wholetone, or modal monochrome of *Pelléas* which caused Strauss to exclaim 'cela manque de Schwung', *Parsifal* has intervened; *Parsifal* that (compared with *Tristan* and *Die Meistersinger*) displays as Einstein says 'a musical language that has become much thinner, more bloodless – it is a work of old age.' Examination of Wagnerian reminiscence in the *music* of *Pelléas* reveals *Parsifal* again and again to be the source; more particularly those areas of Wagner's last opera where thinness and bloodlessness are most in evidence. *Pelléas* takes its plot from the central action of *Tristan* and its subject-matter from *Tristan*'s peripheries; but its musical atmosphere and the means of its musical expression, are not essentially located in *Tristan* at all. The characters of *Pelléas* act

1. It is worth mentioning that even after *Pelléas* Debussy was still interested enough in the *Tristan*-plot to ponder his own operatic version. So late as the 1923 reprint of the first book on him in English, the following promise (originally of 1908) is retained:—
   ' . . . it is announced that M. Albert Carré will shortly produce another work at the Opéra Comique from the pen of the composer of *Pelléas*, which is a series of episodes from "The Story of Tristan". The treatment of this romantic old-world legend will be on totally dissimilar lines from that of the Wagnerian drama. '

out their diminished and *triste* version of the action of *Tristan* in the surroundings of the forests of the Grail.

CHAPTER V

THE INTERLUDES IN PELLEAS

Introduction

The originality — the virtual uniqueness — of *Pelléas* lies in the treatment of voices and words; and here Wagnerian reminiscence is largely a matter of glancing reference, barely caught before it is lost. The interludes, on the other hand, are fertile ground for demonstrating Debussy's use of Wagnerian reminiscence and recreation on as large a scale as he ever does it. They were composed slightly after the main body of the opera, often in a considerable hurry. Debussy's only other large-scale stage-work, *Le Martyre de S. Sébastien*, a work of patent Wagnerian associations, was also written in a hurry, and more than a little unwillingly. The implication seems to be that Debussy turned to Wagner when pressed for time. This might well be true; but, as always, the matter only becomes interesting when, as well as the mere indication of what Debussy 'lifts' and how, it is possible to focus, through these correspondences, on a similarity of evocation and expressive intention between the two. The context of the original provides in almost every case a more significant reason for Debussy's choice than his simply being hurried, even though his hurry might have sent him to these particular sources with greater urgency.

To separate the interludes again from the scenes, as is necessary for discussion, is perhaps to put more weight upon them than they should justly be required to bear. These scene-changing transitions taken by themselves are on the whole decidedly thin; Debussy never attempts a full-scale orchestral panorama like Siegfried's Rhine-Journey or the Transformations in the outer acts of *Parsifal*. In their context, however, the interludes add greatly to the effect of *Pelléas*, and performances of the original version, while perfectly legitimate, seem to me artistically misguided. Without the interludes the perpetual parlando would become monotonous, and the drama would hardly achieve even its present equivocal tragic stature.

ACT I — *1st Interlude* (v.s. pp. 22—5)

This is a scene-change from the depths of the forest and Mélisande and Golaud's first encounter, to 'a room in the castle'. It is in fact a muted Transformation Music, and the reference to Wagner's original is unmistakeable. The soft beginning on strings alone, the gradual incorporation of woodwind and brass, in a march-like movement suggesting the passing of time and space ('Du sieh'st, mein Sohn, zum Raum wird hier die Zeit') as well as place — all are reproduced from *Parsifal* to *Pélleas* (Ex. 1). The characteristic difference is for Wagner to make out of this rhythm a constantly-evolving structural span, while Debussy's use of it is fleeting and transitory — he evokes a march but does not write one. For Parsifal and for his audience transportation into the Castle of the Grail is an overwhelming initiation into a mystery. Debussy's echo of it is much more simply a scene-shift, with Arkel's motif on the trumpets to indicate whose castle is entered. Nevertheless this tenuous evocation of Parsifal's powerful experience gives the interlude a resonance it would otherwise lack.

ACT I — *2nd Interlude* (v.s. pp. 37—9)

The previous scene has touched upon painful emotions — Arkel

Ex. 1a   *Parsifal*, v.s., p. 63

Ex. 1b *Pelléas*, v.s., pp. 24-5

For the gradual incorporation of woodwind and brass, cf. *Parsifal*, m.s., pp. 196-8 with *Pélleas*, m.s., pp. 28-9

the blind old king speaks of Golaud's loneliness since the death of his wife; Pelléas of a beloved friend who is going to die. Frail Mélisande will have to find her place amidst this atmosphere of vague doom and distress. The scene has been the most chastely declamatory even in an opera that does not often require *cantabile* anywhere; as a consequence, the expression of these painful emotions has been perfectly restrained. The characters had repressed their feelings and simply sung their words; the interlude reveals what agonies of desolation lie behind their stylized reserve.

To do so, Debussy has turned to the prelude to Act III of *Parsifal*. The sense of this music is made explicit when, later in the act, it recurs to accompany words. The opening bars (Ex. 2a) describe the decayed state of the community of the Grail, and return when Gurnemanz describes how 'das Bangen wuchs zur höchsten Noth.'[1] 'Ach, sie bedarf des Heiles'[2] can summarize its expressive feeling. The halting chromatic version of the Dresden Amen that begins in bar 12 of the prelude returns rather earlier in the course of the act to accompany Parsifal's account of his years of solitary wandering. Again his first words, 'Der Irrniss und der Leiden Pfade kam ich'[3] may serve as burden of what this music

1. ' . . . the trouble grew to sorest need '. (v.s. p. 233).

2. ' Ah, we have need of succour. ' (Ibid).

3. ' Through error and paths of suffering came I. ' (v.s. p. 229).

Ex. 2a   *Parsifal*, v.s., p. 214

Ex. 2b   *Parsifal*, v.s., p. 214

Ex. 2c   *Parsifal*, v.s., p. 66

Ex. 2d   *Pelléas*, v.s., p. 38

already carries in the prelude. Ex. 2b gives a specimen of this, and 2c gives a few soft bars from the Act I Transformation; 2d is a sample of this particular *Pelléas* interlude. The similarities are a general resemblance of rhythmic movement (with in each case a remote background of slow procession), of scoring for strings, and an intense enharmonic writing, texturally neither quite homophonic nor quite contrapuntal. Compare also the sequential treatment of 2b with bars 5-6 and 7-8 of 2d. While Wagner's sequences accumulate strength through increasing harmonic tension (unquoted here; the succeeding bars will be found as Ex. 11b of Chapter VIII), Debussy's effect is dissipated in the succeeding (unquoted) bars even while the dynamics reach fortissimo, because the harmony loses its tension in weak oscillations. Wagner cumulates, Debussy dissipates.

Ex. 3a   *Parsifal*, v.s., p. 214

Ex. 3b   *Pelléas*, v.s., pp. 38-9

Ex. 3a, which in the prelude to Act III comes between 2a and b, is the motif of Parsifal's wandering (during his narration it is notated in crotchets and quavers, but sounds at the same speed as here). 3b from *Pelléas* echoes the halting syncopated rhythm; the rich tensions of Wagner's harmony are lost in the harmonic undifferentiation of the wholetone scale. In the last bar the syncopation, now in triple time, accompanies Mélisande's motif into the next scene; newly-arrived she strolls with Geneviève before the castle. Various verbal associations strengthen the musical parallels with the opening of *Parsifal* Act III. Mélisande exclaims at the extent of the forests around the castle, and her mother-in-law replies that it is so, and how thick they are, and how much they astonished her when she first arrived . . . 'mais l'on s'y fait si vite . . . Il y a longtemps, il y a longtemps. . . Il y a presque quarante ans que je vis ici.'[1] Retrospectively, then, the function of the interlude has been dual; as well as expressing overtly the emotions that had remained latent in the previous scene, it is now seen to have acted also as a premonition of the sense of desolate wastes and year upon year

1. 'But one so soon grows accustomed . . . it is a long time . . . it is nearly forty years since I came here.'

passing away in the new scene it introduces. The *Parsifal* Act III prelude also describes the passing of many years; the difference is that Geneviève lightly refers to the forty years, whereas in Wagner a substantial time is understood actually to have elapsed since the end of Act II.

The combination in Debussy's interlude of musical similarities with similarities of poetic association testifies to the strength of the impression this music left upon him; while apparently rejecting all vestige of the Wagnerian apparatus he actually as if under some unconscious obligation reproduces extremely characteristic textures and harmonies from a Wagnerian original, in a context of an emotion so explicit that the connection, however unwitting, cannot be fortuitous. His response to this original is intense but notably incomplete. *Parsifal* is the work of an old man whose sensuality even when exhausted always glows with spirituality and whose depiction of spiritual attrition is imbued with an echo of carnal pleasures. Act III in particular is radiant with the paradoxical richness of a renunciation that abandons nothing. This range and depth is beyond Debussy's powers; and anyway, beyond the requirements of his situation. In *Pelléas* he needs only the etiolation.

ACT II – *1st Interlude* (v.s. pp. 72-5)

This interlude follows the scene where Pelléas and Mélisande talk in the castle-gardens, a scene characterized by music of pastoral freshness. The crucial incident – Mélisande losing her marriage-ring in 'la fontaine des aveugles' – is characteristically passed over very lightly in the scene itself. The characters, child-like as they are, understand none of the significance of what they are doing; they agree to tell Golaud the truth, and depart from the scene of the crime. The interlude at first continues the pentatonic-pastoral strain, which gradually gives way to more sombre colouring and whole-tone harmony; her husband's theme is heard as a premonition both of his appearance in the next scene, and symbolically, of the way that he will thwart the lovers' coming together, even though Pelléas and Mélisande remain barely conscious of their love for each other.

The next scene is set in a room in the castle, so again the interlude is a transformation from without to within. Golaud describes how, while out hunting, his horse threw him on the stroke of noon

— the horse fell upon him, but he was oppressed by a weight of doom that he simply cannot comprehend — 'je croyais avoir toute la forêt sur la poitrine. Je croyais que mon coeur était déchiré.'[1] The audience remember that it was on the stroke of noon that Golaud's wife tossed his wedding-ring into the air, and lost it in the 'fontaine des aveugles'. Later in the scene Golaud discovers that the ring is lost, and falls into the first of his jealous rages, sending the cringing Mélisande to recover the ring at all costs. Since she cannot after all tell him the truth she says she thinks she lost it in a cave by the sea.

There is an analogy here with the situation in *Götterdämmerung* Act II regarding Brünnhilde's ring, and, rather than its loss, its appearance on the wrong man's finger and her inference from this that she has been betrayed. In *Götterdämmerung* the situation is of the highest melodramatic tension, whereas the Debussy scene is almost subaqueous, taking place in a miasma which seems hardly to involve directly even the characters who participate in their own events. Nevertheless, in spite of this extreme contrast of method there is a musical connection. The theme that so strikingly characterizes Brünnhilde's sense of betrayal is mainly memorable because of its rhythm. It comes in many guises throughout the scene; Ex. 4a gives the sparest, most easily identifiable version, and 4b the comparable bars from this interlude in *Pelléas*. Certainly if there is a resemblance it is very apposite — but *Götterdämmerung* is unusual ground for Debussy, and the similarity, unlike the echoes of *Parsifal* and *Tristan*, may be no more than coincidental.

A few bars later and this more familiar territory resumes sway. The passage of *Pelléas* given as Ex. 5f though brief is thick with so many Wagnerian sources that their disentanglement becomes a complicated affair. Ex. 5a is a little figure that, though it first characterized an aspect of Kundry in the early pages of Act I, can only be fully understood on its appearance early in Act III. Kundry is now a wretched broken-down creature; her defiance and her voluptuousness are gone, and her one twice-muttered word in the whole of the third act is 'Dienen. . . dienen'. This figure half imitates, half symbolizes, her unaccustomed hesitation and timorous anxiety to please — in a word, her unexpected resemblance to Mélisande.

---

1. "I thought the whole forest lay on my breast. I thought my heart was torn asunder."

83

Ex. 4a   *Götterdämmerung*, v.s., p. 212

Ex. 4b   *Pelléas*, v.s., p. 74

NB: One bar of 4a more or less equals half a bar of 4b in tempo.

Ex. 5a   *Parsifal*, v.s., pp. 220 & 221

Ex. 5b   *Parsifal*, v.s., p. 215

Ex. 5c *Parsifal*, v.s., p. 226

Ex. 5d *Parsifal*, v.s., p. 219

Ex. 5e *Tristan*, v.s., p. 272

5b is one sample of the chord that dominates the early stretches of Act III of *Parsifal;* this two-bar pattern is heard four times in the prelude alone. The first two bars of the *Pelléas* extract are a portmanteau of the hesitant Kundry figure 5a, and the harmony of 5b; as always, Debussy bears lightly what in Wagner is anything but light.

Bars 3-5 of the *Pelléas* extract are a further sample of the intense slow-processional string-writing which Debussy learnt from *Parsifal* (compare Ex. 2a, c and d); they are the same sort of music, conveying the same sort of emotion by the same means. And though one has to admit that Debussy's version is flaccid in comparison with the Wagner — the inner parts are static and the harmonic movement seems unguided — these remarks must not always be criticisms. On the contrary; to be flaccid, static, and unguided is essential to the character of *Pelléas*.

Ex. 5f   *Pelléas*, v.s., p. 75

Bars 7 and 8 of Ex. 5f, with their full violins, recall the passage just after Parsifal has divested himself of his armour, Ex. 5c. But such a two-bar figure, in this tempo, on low strings, recalls also the prelude to Act III of *Tristan*. Bars 6 and 7 of the Debussy sound as if the unforgettable character of the *Tristan*-phrase (Ex. 5e) lay deep in his memory until such time as he had need of it. For the final bars (9-13) of the *Pelléas* extract — a low-lying un-accompanied string-line — there are several precedents in Wagner; 5d, part of the exquisite passage where Gurnemanz restores life to frozen Kundry, is the obvious parallel to draw, seeing how deeply Debussy appears to be involved in this area of *Parsifal*. The examples both come to rest on a soft dominant seventh in its second inversion.

So these thirteen bars of Debussy's interlude — bars on which no especial emotional emphasis can be placed — manifest a plethora of Wagnerian reminiscences and echoes. Their full significance can only be discussed later, when the evidence is complete.

ACT II — *2nd Interlude* (v.s. pp. 103-4)

It is necessary here to make an exception and begin with an example from the previous scene. Before their quarrel about the loss of the ring, Mélisande weeps. Golaud enquires the reason; she doesn't know, and even the audience can but vaguely equate her emotion with the first guilty stirrings of her love for Pelléas. Golaud asks again — 'Can you not fit in with the life we lead here? Is it too sad here?', and continues '. . . it is true this castle is very old and very gloomy . . . very cold and very deep . . . and all who live here are already old. And the landscape too can seem sad, with all these forests, these ancient lightless forests.'[1]

The poetic parallel with the desolate landscape, neglected castle, and the broken-ness of spirit depicted in the opening of Act III of *Tristan* is striking, as is the parallel between the rising phrase that accompanies Golaud's first words — Ex. 6a — and the rising figure that so wonderfully conveys the blankness of outward landscape and inward mental state in the prelude to *Tristan* Act III. This phrase, although it rises, rises so to speak from attenuation to attenuation. No energy is created; listless failure of will has found its perfect musical embodiment. But Tristan, once roused from his amnesia, will proceed from exasperation to exasperation, until at last, purged and exhausted, he dies of his own frenzy. Such galvan-izing into inner activity is outside the scope of the characters in Debussy's opera. Listlessness remains their condition, a lack of will

1. v.s. pp. 90-1.

Ex. 6a   *Pelléas*, v.s., p. 90

Ex. 6b   **Wagner:** *Im Treibhaus*

Ex. 6c   *Pelléas*, v.s., p. 97

Ex. 6d   *Pelléas*, v.s., p. 103

Ex. 6e   *Tristan*, v.s., p. 272

as compulsive as the self-consuming ardours of Wagner's lovers. In *Tristan* this *öd' und leer* phrase always simply evaporates high up on the muted violins, as if Tristan's mortally wounded soul were sighing its last breath. But in *Im Treibhaus*, the third of the *Wesendonk Lieder*, where the three principal themes of the first part of *Tristan* Act III are first used, the phrase always comes to rest, sometimes on a common chord — see Ex. 6b — sometimes unresolved, rather than simply disappearing into the desolate empyrean.

The verbal parallels of Golaud's speech with Mathilde Wesendonk's poem are still more direct than those with Tristan Act III. In the Greenhouse, as in the forests of Allemonde, the spirit wilts under a vague oppression amidst a proliferation of foliage.

Mathilde addresses the palms:-

> Weit in sehendem Verlangen
> Breitet ihr die Arme aus,
> Und umschlinget wahnbefangen
> Öder Leere nicht'ge Graus . . .

> Und wie froh die Sonne schneidet
> Von des Tages leerem Schein,
> Hüllet der, der wahrhaft leidet
> Sich in Schweigens Dunkel ein.[1]

— and here, in the stale language of a fourth-rate mid-nineteenth-century *Lied* is the simple emotion ('Il fait trop triste ici . . . la campagne fait triste aussi . . . avec toutes ces vieilles forêts sans

---

1. ' You spread your arms wide in yearning desire, and embrace in a mad trance the horror of a dreary emptiness . . .
' And as the sun joyfully departs from the empty light of day, so he who truly suffers wraps himself in the darkness of silence. '

lumière') that lies at the heart of *Pelléas*, and that had meanwhile been given such amazing expansion in *Tristan* Act III. The similarity of the musical phrases in Ex. 6a and b, particularly their both coming to rest on a high A major triad, makes a simple identification. Poor Mélisande — like the 'poor plant' which stands for the poem's unpresented but ever-present sufferer, all she can say is 'Our home is not here!'

A few pages later in this scene from *Pelléas* Golaud questions her about the lost ring. Ex. 6c gives her lying answer — 'You know. . . you know. . . the cave down by the sea?' We know it well, for it is a timid echo (the direction is *retenu et hésitant*) of Ex. 6a. The scene ends with Mélisande sent by Golaud (thus blindly forwarding his own fate) with Pelléas to search in this highly symbolic sea-cave for the missing ring that she knows is not there. All these references to the *Treibhaus*-phrase as used at the opening of *Tristan* Act III (given in 6e) fuse in the first two bars (6d) of the interlude that follows Mélisande's weeping exit. Again Wagner has provided a rich original of emotion-evoking music, from which Debussy remembers only the thin glimmer that will be enough for his purpose.

The interlude continues with similar material, interwoven with snatches of the pastoral music from the fountain-scene when the ring was lost, which gives way to a brief *lent* passage — Ex. 7a — before the purely atmospheric evocation of the dark seashore in front of the cave. The rhythm of 7a, and its two-bar pattern, are derived from 6d; there is consequently a relationship with all the Wagner sources given in Ex. 6. But now the harmony has changed; each of the four bars of 7a lingers on the *Tristan*-chord itself. Both Ex. 6d and 7a are variants of the first half of Mélisande's motif (given as 7b for reference). In 6d it is subject to her husband's inner desolation, represented by the *öder Leere* harmony from *Im Treibhaus* and *Tristan* Act III. Now the same fragment is subject to the connotations of the chord, four times repeated, that expresses the yearning of Wagner's lovers. The chord indicates more explicitly than ever they do themselves the nature of Pelléas's and Mélisande's feelings for each other; and the motif, in its very limpness and instinct for camouflage, shows how subject is its owner to even the feeblest domination, and how vulnerable to the slightest breath of fate.

Ex. 7a   *Pelléas*, v.s., p. 103

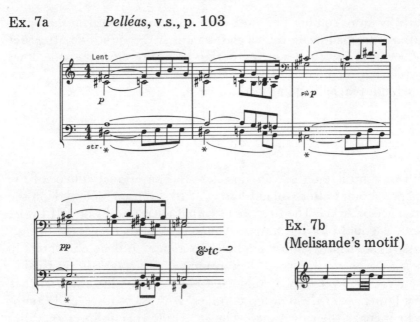

Ex. 7b
(Melisande's motif)

The function of the interlude is to reveal to the audience that, unknown to themselves, the lovers are lovers, and to intimate what kind of lovers they are. This intimation is endorsed in the ensuing scene, when, alone together at night on the seashore, a flood of moonlight illuminating them one to another makes them become shy and awkward: they are both frightened at what is revealed, and Mélisande's final words, 'Laissez-moi; je préfère marcher seule. . .' rather put romance in its place. The contrast this scene presents with the moonlit irradiation of the lovers in Act I of *Die Walküre* will be discussed more fully in the next chapter.

ACT III

There is less to say about the interludes in Act III. The second and third (v.s. pp. 147-9 and 157-8) are transitional passages from one scene to another; absolutely adequate for their purpose, they are musically very thin, and offer no point of contact with Wagner. The interlude after the first scene (pp. 140-1) when Golaud has interrupted the lovers as they exchange tremulous raptures in the

dark, is more sombre in mood than any music heard in the opera
so far, foreshadowing the elegiac strain of the interlude after Act
IV scene ii. Its touches of Wagnerian harmony show the same kind
of relation to the original as that already discussed in Ex. 7, now
much diluted, and adding nothing new.

ACT IV

The central interlude in this act—the emotional climax of the
opera[1]—comes after Golaud has violently abused Mélisande in the
presence of Arkel. The first scene ended with Arkel's line 'If I were
God, I would pity the hearts of men', a line that gives the opera's
passive fatalism its most explicit utterance. All the characters in
Pelléas, even the lovers in their principal scene, remain swathed in
their vacuous yet impenetrable self-ness; the nihilistic inference is
that human beings can never 'connect' with each other, and cannot
even manage their own pity. The interlude that follows amplifies
the reverberation of 'Si j'étais Dieu, j'aurais pitié du coeur des
hommes'. The first nine bars (v.s. p. 220) are the nearest approach
in the opera to tragic expression, an unusually sustained attempt
to put the action and its characters and its music on a more grand
and less private footing. It is not sustained for long: the grave fervour disintegrates into amorphous wholetone harmony,.which in
turn gradually subsides into Ex. 8a. A few quiet bars—Ex. 9a—
follow, and a flurried and transitory climax fading away as rapidly
as it rises into a repeat of 8a. This phrase strikingly recalls the solo
timpani, soft brass, and low pizzicati of Parsifal's arrival early in

Ex. 8a   *Pelléas*, v.s., p. 222

1. Its position was emphasized in the original production, where it led into the principal
   scene between Mélisande and Pélleas. The scene actually following, Yniold's encounter
   with the stone and the sheep, represents Maeterlinck at his most vapid.

Act IV

Ex. 8b   *Parsifal*, v.s., pp. 222-3

Ex. 9a   *Pelléas*, v.s., p. 222

Ex. 9b   *(Tristan)*

Ex. 9c   *Tristan*, v.s., p. 263

Act III (Ex. 8b) particularly as this phrase is heard three times in all. While 9a (which comes between the two appearances of 8a) is a decoration of the unforgettable first two chords of *Tristan*—9b gives them transposed to make the connection clear. The final chord of 9a recalls, rather, the opening of *Tristan* as it recurs in a very different context, at the end of Act II after the lovers are discovered and Marke has delivered his woeful monologue. To Marke's final question,

> Den unerforschlich tief geheimnisvollen Grund
> Wer macht der Welt ihn kund?[1]

Tristan's reply[2] is simply Ex. 9c, the opening bars of the opera with a new quasi-resolution, marked *, at the end of each phrase. The Debussy reminiscence also touches upon this quasi-resolution, memorable because the *Tristan*-motif does not often resolve onto a consonance.

So in a brief space in the climactic interlude of Debussy's opera, two further references to the early part of *Parsifal* Act III enclose a reminiscence of a peculiarly poignant moment in *Tristan*. Already discussion of *La Damoiselle élue* has shown the importance for Debussy of Parsifal's arrival, and how deeply the music of that scene has imprinted itself in his memory. I would suggest that Tristan's answer to Marke's question, the attitude question and answer indicate, and their context in the drama, might well evoke an even more intimate quiver of response. The interruption of lovers, the question that can never be answered, the things that can never be told—this is all crucial to *Pelléas*. Tristan is in fact perfectly explicit in the articulation of his most rarified as of his most

---

1. ' Who shall tell the world the deep, secret, inscrutable cause? '
2. ' Oh King, that I cannot tell thee; and what you ask, that can'st thou never undergo. '

passionate feelings; the hesitation, the stammering on the brink of the void that he claims for himself belong much more truthfully to his counterpart in Debussy's opera.

Conclusion

The echoes and reminiscences of Wagner, both specific and diffused, that abound in the *Pelléas*-interludes, testify to an absorption so thorough on Debussy's part that his reaction against his favourite-but-hated composer appears disingenuous indeed. Put baldly, Debussy is taking Wagnerian *minutiae* that appeal deeply to him both in themselves and for their context, and re-employing them, less or more transformed, sometimes for the same purposes sometimes not, in a style so different that there would at first seem no basis for comparison. This strange trait (it is too wayward and involuntary to be called a process, let alone a technique) provides an unexpected precedent for the re-composition' made familiar by Stravinsky, who, defending his stylistic plundering as a creative activity, speaks of suffering from 'some rare form of kleptomania' – whatever he loves he wants to make his own. It is as characteristic of Stravinsky that he should thus superbly acknowledge his practice, as it is of Debussy that it should be so covert. The ambiguity of his fascination with and rejection of Wagner makes his conscious attitudes defensive, thus preventing direct enjoyment and use of Wagner's riches. But his composition, however unconsciously, is wiser than his attitudes; and in it he *does* allow the access (be it never so disguising and diminishing), and succeeds in lifting many precious rareties; so subtly, moreover, that it would seem that the loss has not so far been noticed.

CHAPTER VI

WAGNERIAN MINUTIAE IN PELLEAS

1. *Introduction*

The Interludes in *Pelléas* have been treated separately not only because they lend themselves to separate treatment by virtue of their function as interludes, but also because the references they show to Wagner are susceptible of analysis which yields some kind of cogent interpretation. I now want to deal with Wagnerian *minutiae* in the vocal portions of *Pelléas*, and will find it necessary for the first time really to analyze "the smallest particles" of which Wölfflin spoke.[1]

The particular danger in such analysis is of that failure of taste which makes much more of the marginal elements held in common by various works of art, than of the stylistic differentiations which should render them strictly speaking incomparable. This doubt is put generally by Edgar Wind, in discussing historians of art, including Wölfflin, who ' methodically developed an exquisite skill in skimming off the top of a work of art without necessarily making contact with its imaginative forces, often even shunning that contact because it might disturb the lucid application of a fastidious technique '.

This chapter, therefore, runs the risk both of claiming more significance in superficial and passing resemblances than in profound and lasting differences; and, in doing so, of ignoring the radically dissimilar expressive aims behind these stylistic differences. So it is important to bear in mind the general truths that will necessarily be lost in a detailed discussion. In considering the Wagnerian *minutiae* (of harmony, melody, orchestral usage, word-setting, etc.) within the vocal portions of Debussy's opera, it must always be remembered that it is precisely in these portions that what is quintessentially *Debussyan* is most in evidence; here is the conscious resistance to Wagner's methods that Debussy himself speaks of when he writes, while composing the earliest

1. See p. 21.

draft of Act IV scene iv, ' the ghost of old Klingsor, alias R. Wagner, appeared at a turning of one of the bars so I tore the whole thing up and struck off on a new line with a little compound of phrases I thought more characteristic . . . '.

Moreover in order to pursue this kind of analysis, everything psychologically expressive has to be resisted; it is drained off, as it were, into the discussion of the interludes and the comparison of the plot of *Tristan* and *Pelléas* that has occupied the preceding two chapters. This chapter is confined to a residue of impressionistic, and even random, musical connections—*merely* musical, indeed, in the sense that an explanation cannot be found to produce more significance of meaning than a passing flicker of resemblance in one musical element or another. In these more marginal Wagnerian reminiscences the attribution of interpretative significance would, on the whole, be risky when it is not entirely factitious—though a continuous theme does emerge in considering Act V.

2. *Minutiae in Acts I-IV*

ACT I

Ex. 1a i *sounds* very like *Parsifal* but is curiously difficult to attach to a source there. The closest approximation to establishing a reminiscence is to show these chords as parallel ninths a semitone apart (a ii), and take a passage and its abstract from Wagner (1b i-ii) where the ninths slide in parallel major thirds. 1c, the first appearance, a couple of bars before 1a, of Mélisande's theme, might perhaps be suggested (especially since it is at the same pitch) in the first bars of the *Parsifal* extract — see 1d. But after Debussy's direct use of this same passage in *La Damoiselle*,[1] this connection is somewhat devious — and anyway the so-Wagnerian arrival of the second chord of 1a becomes immediately Debussyan by the added D in the harmony.

The solitary oboe note which introduces the defenceless Mélisande to Golaud has an ancestor in *Siegfried* Act III, where Brünnhilde is 'ohne Schutz und Schirm, ohne Trutz ein trauriges

1. Chapter II Ex. 12c.

Ex. 1a i   *Pelléas*, v.s., p. 2

Ex. 1a ii

Ex. 1b i   *Parsifal*, v.s., p. 232

Ex. 1b ii

Ex. 1c   *Pelléas*, v.s., p. 1

Ex. 1d

Weib!'[1]. The similarity here is that of a musical simile (a sudden check in a previously continuous texture, the oboe note twice emerging as a poignant indication of female distress) rather than its specific musical context (Ex. 2). But as Debussy proceeds his

Ex. 2   *Siegfried*, v.s., p. 311

content, too, can be traced to a different Wagnerian source, the opening of Act III of *Parsifal*. Both *Pelléas* and Wagner are given in Ex. 3; the relationship between the two chords of Ex. 3b, over six bars of *Parsifal*, is in the last bar of the Debussy extract repro-

1. '... without protection or shelter, a poor defenceless woman!'

Ex. 3a   *Pelléas*, v.s., pp. 4-5 (vocal part omitted)

Ex. 3b   *Parsifal*, v.s., p. 215 — skeleton of bars 6-12

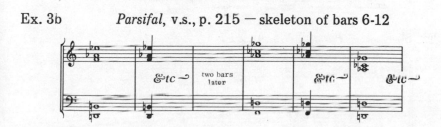

duced in a mere half-bar. The chords, apart from enharmonic
differences and differences of lay-out, are at the same pitch —
their first occurrence (Debussy bars 5 and 6) had used the identical
chords a fourth lower. The difference between a and b is that
Wagner's chords are separated by thematic matter presented in
terms of a harmonic *progress* from the one to the other, whereas
in Debussy they simply *sound*, as such, juxtaposed together without any connection. This is neatly symbolized by the way the bass-
notes that give them their linguistic function in the Wagner are
absent from Debussy's use — his chords have no anchor and no
rationale.

Ex. 4a   Ex. 4b
Pelléas, v.s., p. 11   *Parsifal*, v.s., p. 174

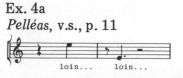

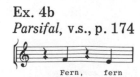

Ex. 4 presents a simple similarity in word-setting – questioned about their origins, Mélisande and Kundry both repeat the word 'far' in a disembodied, vaguely uneasy-making way. Ex. 5 is more complex and less satisfactory. 5a, Golaud recounts his hunting; his characteristic nervous rhythm recalls that of the Kundry-Klingsor relation in Acts I and II of *Parsifal*. Act III in fact provides the example most similar in harmony to the extract from *Pelléas* (5b); but the more characteristic form of the rhythm is shown in 5c, in both its common and triple time versions.

Ex. 5a *Pelléas*, v.s., p. 17

Ex. 5b *Parsifal*, v.s., p. 217

Ex. 5c i *Parsifal*, v.s., p. 207

Ex. 5c ii *Parsifal*, v.s., p. 210

Ex. 6a is a further reference by Debussy to the music accompanying Parsifal's disarming, early in Act III (6b); unlike his earlier one[1] this recreation attempts to emulate something of Wagner's sublimity. It is the first of Arkel's solemn pronouncements (it touches a decided note of grave bathos): 'Il n'arrive peut-être pas d'évènements inutiles'.[2] That Debussy's setting

1. Chapter II Ex. 10.

2. ' Perhaps no event is useless. '

recreates the passage from *Parsifal* is immediately plain—the pedal
E, underpinning a move from E major to the chord E G B♭ D, the

Ex. 6a   *Pelléas*, m.s., p. 38 (vocal line omitted)

Ex. 6b   *Parsifal*, m.s., p. 698

similarity in mood and pace, and above all the orchestral sonority.
The melodic lines (which have in themselves no similarity) are
given in both passages to a unison mass of all the strings except
the basses, and this mass is supported by horns, trombones, and
tuba—in Debussy trumpets and a drum roll too, in Wagner bassoons
and clarinets. A sonorous near-tutti like this is rare in *Pelléas*.
Taking the differences of melodic line into account, Wagner even
at his slower pace takes two bars to Debussy's one—and the
subsequent course of the *Pelléas* passage is typically towards
flaccidity and fragmentation, whereas Wagner continues and intensifies. So direct an instance would seem to suggest that this similarity is 'meaningful' in the same way as the Wagnerian reminiscences
in the *Pelléas* interludes; but it is more plausible to put it under the
head, not so much of random connections, as of that kind in which
a generalized impression of mood (in this case a vaguely oppressive
significance and grandeur) is remembered from the original and

employed in its new context almost as conventional usage or
affect.

However, the next example is given as a parody of the kind of
connection that really does indicate a meaning. Ex. 7a and b—five
bars in *Pelléas* on an added-sixth of C, like the flower-maiden
passage in *Parsifal* II. Ex. 7c shows them as an inversion of each
other, with the four added-sixth notes in common, *Parsifal* adding
F#, and *Pelléas* B♭, then F# too. A verbal parallel too—Arkel
sings 'Viens un peu plus près . . .', the maidens sing 'so bleib'
nicht fern . . .'—but perhaps this sort of closeness is far-fetched!

Ex. 7a   *Pelléas*, v.s., p. 34 (vocal part omitted)

Ex. 7b   *Parsifal*, v.s., p. 143

Ex. 7c

ACT II

Scene three of this act presents resemblances simultaneously to
Die Walküre Act I and the Norn scene in the *Götterdämmerung*
Prologue. His characters' situation 'devant une grotte' has elicited
from Debussy one of the musical images that Wagner uses for the
Norns as they sing beneath Brünnhilde's rock—see Ex. 8a. and b.
The resemblance in chord-content is small, but the resemblance as a
musical image is obvious. From this a more technical statement of
their similarity can be drawn, in describing them both as a pattern
formed by a semitonal trill ornamenting a bare fifth, as shown in
8c; Debussy's a semitone down, Wagner's a semitone up. The main
difference now is that while Debussy makes an atmospheric
chordal blur (to this accompaniment Pelléas sings ' Il fait si noir
que l'entrée de la grotte ne se distingue plus du reste de la nuit '[1])
in common time, Wagner articulates (in triple time) a *theme*—the
Norns' ashy version of Loge's fire-motif.

Ex. 8a   *Pelléas*, v.s., p. 105

Ex. 8b   *Götterdämmerung*, v.s., p. 12

Ex. 8c i Wagner   Ex. 8c ii Debussy

Ex. 9a, a few moments later in the same scene of *Pelléas*, comes
more closely into the realm of the Norns—and here the movement
is now in $\frac{6}{4}$, bringing the rhythm as well as the other elements into
line with the Wagnerian original—the beginning of *Götterdämmerung* (9b—the phrase is quoted here on its second appearance,
in D♭ minor, to correspond with Debussy's C♯ minor). In Wagner's

1. 'It is so dark that you can't distinguish the mouth of the cave from the night.'

Ex. 9a   *Pelléas*, v.s., p. 108

Ex. 9b   *Götterdämmerung*, bars 10-12

terms this passage of course refers to the emergent world at the beginning of the whole *Ring*. Not however in Debussy's; for him the primeval diatonicism of *Rheingold* has less intensity of interest, less atmospheric *frisson*, than this shadowy version that augurs a world at its ending. Wagner achieves the weary dustiness of the Norn-scene most particularly in the threads of ninths and elevenths that stand at once for the sisters' spinning and the dusk that they perpetually inhabit—Ex. 10a is a characteristic specimen of these chord-formations, which, recurring throughout the scene, give it a different harmonic 'feel' from anything else in Wagner. The grotto-scene in *Pelléas* employs this imagery—see Ex. 10b, i and ii— though these chords of altered ninths and elevenths are still presented as slow tremoli in the manner of both the Debussy and Wagner passages in Ex. 8.

Ex. 10a   *Götterdämmerung*, v.s., p. 2

Ex. 10b i
Pelléas, v.s., p. 108, last bar

Ex. 10b ii
Pelléas, v.s., p. 109, bar 3

Both scenes take place in tenebrous gloom, pointed and sharpened by verbal references to light—the Norns' questions to each other, 'Welch Licht leuchtet dort?'; 'Dämmert der Tag?'[1]; and the perpetual dulled flicker of the fire-music in the background: and Pelléas's description (to the chords of 10b i) of what would happen if a little light were lit within the grotto—'on dirait que la voûte est couverte d'étoiles, comme le ciel'.[2] For this situation of murkiness and anxiety, depicted by imitation of itself and reference to its opposite, Wagner has found the strong musical images which Debussy uses in his customary diffused fashion. Or rather, if Wagner has found a musical symbol for his situation,

1 'What light starts up?' 'Dawns the day?'

2. 'It looks as though the vault is full of stars like the sky'.

Debussy converts this into something atmospheric, something which creates mood and 'impression'. The technical difference between the 'symbolic' and the 'impressionistic' is that the one carries a syntactical and thematic burden, while the other has no function except to effect atmosphere-painting. Ex. 8b was thematic whereas 8a was a blur; similarly the Wagner half of Ex. 9 is latent both with thematic content and grammatical function, whereas the Debussy in the same example is complete, or rather incomplete, in itself, with no other musical capacity than to illustrate a scene and a mood. Even the ninths and elevenths of 10a have thematic content, relating clearly to the whole nexus of motifs in the *Ring* built on thirds, including that of the ring itself—in 10b they are, again, passing, colouristic, neither thematic nor motivic nor part of any harmonic movement.

And now, the coming of the light; it is as if the Norn-scene gave way, not to the gradual dawn and 'Voller Tag'[1] of the mature love-music of Siegfried and Brünnhilde, but to the sudden shaft of 'Vollmond'[2] by whose light respectively her cousins and his parents are clearly revealed to each other for the first time, and realize that they are lovers. The situation both in *Pelléas* and *Die Walküre* is that the audience's sympathy so extends to the adulterous couple that the injured husband becomes supernumerary. Golaud and Hunding have pronounced features in common—their roughness, heavy strength, harshness towards their wives and aggression towards the men they imagine to be their wives' lovers. Though the means of their death are hardly part of the present conjunction, both Siegmund and Pelléas are in the end struck down by the avenging sword of the outraged husband. Musically, Hunding and Golaud are characterized by the same kind of figure, sharply articulated, abrupt, potentially explosive; Ex. 11 gives typical examples. I don't urge a direct resemblance here; enough to note that similarity of character produces general similarity of musical image; one that perhaps could occur to any composer requiring to depict a man who is at once a strong warrior and a baleful husband.

What does give these scenes something more of a connection has already been mentioned—the device of employing a flood of moon-

1. 'Full daylight'. *(Götterdämmerung v.s. p. 20.)*
2. 'Full moonlight' *(Die Walküre v.s. p. 52).*

106

Ex. 11a   *Walküre,* v.s., p. 16

Ex. 11b   *Pelléas,* v.s., p. 76

light to reveal the emotions of the characters as well as their faces. The moonlight shows Pelléas and Mélisande, as it does Siegmund and Sieglinde, that they are lovers. The similarity established, the differences have at once to be urged that render such a comparison almost untenable, so greatly do they indicate the divergent intentions and achievements of the two composers. For Wagner's lovers, moonlight brings self-discovery, mutual awareness of mutual passion, and an ecstatic embracing of fate; the stream of lyricism it unlocks is unique in the *Ring* tetralogy. In Debussy the rapture of the moonlight is but four bars long (v.s. p. 111), and it illumines, as well as the lovers, the disquieting sight of three sleeping paupers. From this moment onwards Pelléas and Mélisande speak in still softer whispers; and the music, far from growing progressively in rich explicitness, thins into almost total attenuation. To a second occurrence of the moonlight-music Mélisande resists Pelléas's attempt to take her arm—'Laissez-moi; je préfère marcher seule . . .' (p. 114), and with the last words of the act ('Nous reviendrons un autre jour') and a final echo of the moonlight-strain, the chaste and frightening rapture of the episode has already receded into an inaccessible past. The musical direction—' en retenant et en s'affaiblissant jusqu'à la fin '—has poetic and dramatic felicity over and above its technical· instruction for the performance of these last evanescent bars. The audience sees clearly that the lovers are lovers, but they themselves are rendered still more reticent and separate by the experience.

This resemblance rather in plot than in musical details returns to the larger vagaries of Chapter IV. The connection between Wagner and Debussy as shown in this comparison of their treatment of moonlight, guilty lovers, and baleful husbands, fits plausibly into the view that in the treatment of a similar action, Wagner makes for amplitude, Debussy for attrition; Wagner for emotional fullness, Debussy for its negation. Golaud as violent husband has the threatening aspect of Hunding without the power; as injured husband he has the feebleness of Marke without the gentleness and nobility. Similarly Pelléas and Mélisande have the fullness neither of the spiritual-erotic, like the lovers in *Tristan*, nor yet the vernal-erotic of Siegmund and Sieglinde. It is *they* who should be brother and sister!—indeed Golaud himself touches on something extraordinarily unrealized in the ostensible subject of the opera when he says in Act V 'Ils s'étaient embrassés comme des petits enfants . . . ils étaient frère et soeur . . .'.

However the music for all this latter part of the scene in *Pelléas* is entirely unWagnerian. As the moon sheds its light, it is not only the shadowy echoes of the Norns (as detailed in Exx. 8-10) that are dispersed, but any relation to Wagner except that of stylistic and expressive antithesis.

ACT III

At the end of the first scene, the flirtation of Pelléas and Mélisande is discovered by Golaud; Ex. 12a accompanies her first apprehension of her husband's arrival—'J'entends un bruit de pas . . . Laisse-moi!' Extraordinary to find in these two chords, so scurried that the ear can hardly register their relation to each other except by lingering on them, a reproduction of that same passage early in Act III of *Parsifal* whose strong effect upon Debussy I have already mentioned.[1] Previously he had used its rhythm, mood, and orchestral lay-out; here (as shown in Ex. 12b) he uses only its harmony; the earlier reminiscence was the more complex, in that it sought to reproduce the total context of the original—here the resemblance is merely that the harmony, at the same pitch, is identical.

Ex. 12a
Pelléas, v.s., p. 137
(voice part omitted)

Ex. 12b
Parsifal, v.s., pp. 222-3
(condensed)

Ex. 13a
Pelléas, v.s., p. 139

Ex. 13b
Parsifal, v.s., p. 144

Ex. 13c   Hagen-harmony in *Götterdämmerung*

However, the principal Wagnerian *minutiae* in this act come from rather an unexpected source; they show Golaud's Hunding-aspect intensified in malevolence to assume an unmistakeable reflection of the thematic characterization of Hagen in *Götterdämmerung*. Ex. 13a gives the highly-coloured harmonization of Golaud's motif as he rebukes his wife and his half-brother for playing like children in the dark. Here it is the last two chords that present something new, and so sharply recognizable that its use in

1. See Ch. V Ex. 8.

Wagner can immediately be specified. Even a passing glance in the flowermaid music is haunting—13b—but the most characteristic and memorable use is associated with Hagen's watch in *Götterdämmerung* Act I and his dream-converse with Alberich which opens Act II. Ex. 13c quotes it at the same pitch as the *Pelléas* example; the first chord is in Wagner a ninth and in Debussy a seventh, but here the G# held for the first four crochets of the bar gives the illusion that it is still the root of the two chords in question. Ex. 14a, four bars later, recalls another memorable Hagen-harmony, now the vassal-summoning rather than the brooding Hagen, first heard very starkly as the day dawns on which his brooding will end—Ex. 14b. This striking harmony is also associated in *Götterdämmerung* with the presentation of the Valhalla-motif in terms of Tarnhelm chords, a motivic pun that occurs at especially solemn or chilling moments in the drama; Ex. 14c is one of five occurrences in Waltraute's narration; the others are all associated with Hagen and Alberich.[1] Another, rather dubious, connection might be traced between the triplet figures that creep stealthily upwards through the texture of Gutrune's theme before Hagen's Act I soliloquy, through his own music after it, and the repeat of this before the appearance of Alberich at the beginning of Act II.[2] The triplet scales in the vault-scene

Ex. 14a
Pelléas, v.s., p. 139

Ex. 14b
Götterdämmerung, v.s., p. 141

Ex. 14c   *Götterdämmerung*, v.s., p. 104

1. *Götterdämmerung* v.s. pp. 86; 101; 103-4; 139.
2. *Ibid.*, pp. 86; 88; 131.

(Act III scene ii) of *Pelléas* creep downwards through a common-time texture whose performing indication is 'lourd ét sombre'.[1] This, more even than Ex. 8, is a resemblance of musical image rather than musical execution; however, Exx.13 and 14 do seem to me to show direct reference to Hagen's music, even though only three crotchets' length of Debussy's music is involved. The reason is that both these progressions, so sharply focused in sound that they are not easily forgotten, are unique in *Pelléas*; moreover they are employed in *Götterdämmerung* with powerful emphasis as the musical expression of the drama at moments of crucial intensity. It is wiser simply to point out that Debussy has briefly recalled the sound-characteristics of these Hagen-harmonies than to try to establish a putative 'influence' of *Götterdämmerung* upon *Pelléas* (though indeed there are parallel features between Golaud and Hagen). But whether or not there is any aptness in their doing so, these three crotchets of Debussy's music manifest a capacity for the reproduction of remembered sounds in Wagner that amounts almost to citation.

Ex. 15a   *Pelléas*, v.s., pp. 184-5

Ex. 15a is another instance of harmony seemingly unique in *Pelléas*; surprising, since it is built directly out of the wholetone scale. Augmented triads like this immediately recall the augmented-triad music in the *Ring*, notably Loge's shifty and shiftless fire-music. The version of this in the Norn-scene (15b) shows the similarity in sound clearly, though the outer chords are not augmented triads—it lies in the rise and fall of the bass of a minor third, which by creating an illusion of contrary motion prevents what is in fact a semitonal parallel shift from sounding it. Of course augmented harmony in Wagner is *intended* to be elusive, wandering, trackless; in Debussy the wholetone harmony which develops from it is, in all its indecision, deliberately normative.

1. *Pelléas* v.s. p. 143.

Ex. 15b   *Götterdämmerung*, v.s., p. 8

ACT IV

In the scene of Golaud's jealousy, Debussy turns away from the *Ring* towards Klingsor for some of his characterising devices. This is seen especially in the use of numerous little vocal inter-jections which give a maniacal frenzy both to Klingsor's ambitious visions and to Golaud's self-destructive fury. The main similarity of situation is that they are tormenting the women in their possession—Golaud pulls Mélisande around by the hair, Klingsor wreaks spells, threats and compulsions upon Kundry. His repertory of ejaculations includes single instances of 'Wie', 'ja ja', 'pfui!', and 'so!'[1]; several 'He!'s and 'Ho!'s[2]; and no less than six cases of 'Ha!'[3], and six also of 'Ha ha!'[4]. It would be absurd to catalogue these things with such punctilious relish were it not for the fact that Klingsor's vocal self-projection has left its mark upon Debussy's characterization of Golaud. In the five pages (v.s. 213-7) of Golaud's frenzy there are four of these nervous 'ah! ah!' interjections, and the more sustained speech is, like Klingsor's, full of imperative phrases—'Ici!'; 'Allez vous-en!'; 'En avant! en arrière!' and so forth—which lend themselves to vehement articulation. Moreover the musical momentum set up is at some points similar, as can be seen in Ex. 16a and b. Here, however, the momentum is the only point of resemblance, and even so Wagner's tempo is so much more solid than Debussy's that the similarity is greater on paper than in aural effect. The substantial influence of

1. *Parsifal* v.s. pp. 124; 113; 111; 121.
2. *Ibid.* pp. 112; 124; 120.
3. *Ibid.* pp. 110; 114; 119; 120; 121; 123.
4. *Ibid.* pp. 111; 112; 117; 121; 122; 124.

Klingsor upon this scene of *Pelléas* is that Klingsor's word-setting
provides a rhetoric of uneasy violence, anxiety, sadistic mockery,
and droll or agonized self-laceration, which Debussy grafts on to
his essentially external, Mussorgskian depiction of Golaud, as his
rage requires.

Ex. 16a   *Parsifal*, v.s., p. 120 (voice part omitted)

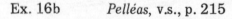

Ex. 16b   *Pelléas*, v.s., p. 215

Ex. 17 shows that several orchestral usages in Yniold's scene
with the sheep have possibly been remembered from the opening
of *Tristan* Act II. Here above all there is no connection to be made

113

in subject-matter! In common is the employment of these accompanimentary orchestral devices—compare 17a and d; b and e; c and f i and ii—which run through both scenes as an image of the spread of twilight, night thickening, a rustling and blurring of the musical texture.

Ex. 17a
Tristan, m.s., p. 311

Ex. 17b
Tristan, m.s., pp. 311-12

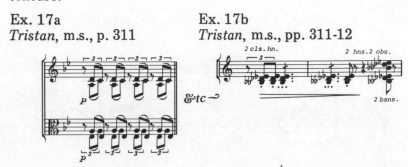

Ex. 17c   *Tristan*, m.s., pp. 333-4

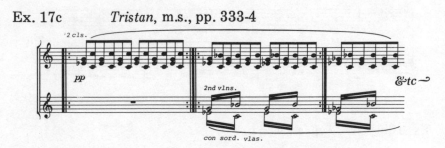

Ex. 17d   *Pelléas*, m.s., p. 313

Ex. 17e

Ex. 17f i   *Pelléas*, m.s., p. 315

Ex. 17f ii   *Pelléas*, m.s., p. 315

The next example goes to the centre of *Tristan* Act II, and to the love-scene in *Pelléas*—but the principal Wagnerian reference in Debussy's music is rather to Brangäne than to the heroic lovers whom she serves. Ex. 18a gives Pelléas's 'twelve bars of ecstasy'[1]; the features that mark it as a reminiscence of Brangäne's two islands in the flow of the *Tristan* love-duet, are the harp arpeggio in bar 7, and the snatch of melody in bars 8-9, repeated in 10-11.

Ex. 18a   *Pelléas*, m.s., pp. 350-52

1. See p. 72.

The first six bars of this passage dwell upon the *Tristan*-chord itself; the chord in the seventh bar is the second chord of the *Tristan*-phrase with (as so often when Debussy employs this progression) the note added that makes the original seventh a ninth. This chord is spread out on the harp in a way recalling the five harp arpeggii that introduce Brangäne's first intermezzo. Ex. 18c shows one of these, and 18b shows the relation of bars 1-7 of the *Pelléas* extract to the *Tristan*-phrase. Debussy's elision of the

Ex. 18c   *Tristan*, m.s., p. 569

original now goes to the end of Brangäne's intermezzo, her 'Habet Acht!' which is used to conclude her second as well as her first interruption. Apart from one small verbal change the two are identical, except that the second is a semitone higher than the first. 18d gives the second version simply because in G rather than F# it also *looks* like the Debussy that, in both keys, it so resembles in sound. The resemblances lie between the flowing phrases in the first three bars and bars 8-11 of the Debussy; and the C major added sixth which forms the single highpoint of Wagner's phrase (in bar 4) and in Debussy is also the highpoint, lingered on for the best part of four bars. A more general resemblance is the loss of the singer's line, as it merges with a singing orchestral line, in both passages. Finally, at each ending of Brangäne's warning there is a perfect cadence, the first time in G♭ major, the second in G major; they stand out strongly in a work which proceeds by notably avoiding the V-I progression. The last chord of Ex. 18a is a specific promise of an E major resolution, and this promise is the final Wagner-reminiscence in this Debussy passage—but one is jolted out of the carefully prepared full close, for this is the moment when sharp-eared Mélisande has heard, more carefully than her lover's rapt self-communings, Golaud's footsteps crackling the dead leaves[1]. Thus Debussy's twelve bars are a compacted

Ex. 18d   *Tristan*, m.s., pp. 614/5-18
               (wind instruments sustain harmony throughout)

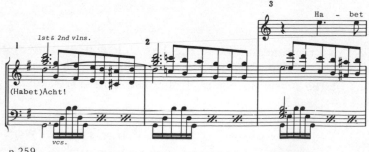

1. v.s. p.259.

version of Brángäne's music in the *Tristan* love-duet. However, the central part of her first intermezzo, which employs the richer strains of the music proper to Isolde and Tristan (v.s. pp. 216-7), he has jettisoned.

It could be argued, even while the reference in this passage of *Pelléas* to Brángäne's music is granted, that this kind of Wagnerian reminiscence in Debussy does not provide enough scope to call for, let alone to justify, such interpretative speculations as these. The question is, whether a use of the original music bears also some kind of endorsement, explicit or implicit, of the original's verbal, dramatic, atmospheric and emotional content. It is a question that has to be re-decided ever and again on the likelihoods of every individual case. The range is a wide one between on the one hand deliberate use (whether unconscious or not) by Debussy of Wagner's music in an expressive context common to them both, however different the intention and result; and on the other the random, the accidental or even the irresponsible use of a Wagnerian original—impressionistic rather than deliberate (whether conscious or not), often rendering it linguistically nonsensical and only comprehensible in terms of colour and sonority—with no possible significance of emotional correlation between the two. Many of the examples in this section on *minutiae* belong well towards the centre of this range; Ex. 18 is the most ambiguous. It might be felt that such a resemblance is merely an 'atmospheric' borrowing on Debussy's part, shedding no light on any meaning, but only upon the capacity of the mind to retain and reproduce new guises of unexpected sources in inappropriate surroundings. On the other hand, if once I feel obliged to account more seriously for the reminiscence being there at all, I must produce the explanation, the speculative interpretation that, though it eventually seems far-fetched or even 'literary', in fact arises directly from apprehensions as to the nature of music and what it can do.

But there is hardly any interpretative significance in the way that the end of *Pelléas* Act IV recalls the end of the first Act of *Die Walküre*. A comparison of the last 15 bars of the Wagner[1] with the last 16 of the Debussy[2] will show the extent, and the limits, of the similarity. As a violent curtailing gesture the likeness is strong, but almost nothing in detail, except generalities like the rushing quavers, the bars of powerful syncopation for tutti orchestra, and the violence of the final suspension, which in both cases minimizes the audibility of its resolution. Again the characteristic difference of effect makes the similarity almost risible—Wagner's culmination is effortlessly strong, the climax of a long journey towards it, whereas Debussy's arises in only

1. Eulenburg m.s. pp. 242-4.
2. M.s. pp. 363-4.

fourteen bars from *pp* to *fff*, explodes with febrile vehemence, and collapses with a nervous thwack. Hunding has struck down 'frère et soeur' before they've had time to recognize each other for what they are.

3. ACT V – A *Tristan*-vein in *Pelléas*

'On dirait que son âme a froid pour toujours . . .'; 'Kalt und starr! Diessmal hielt ich sie wohl für todt'.[1] These are the words that accompany the passages that form Ex. 19. The Debussy comes just after Arkel has said these words over Mélisande as she sleeps; the passage from *Parsifal* comes after Gurnemanz has descried Kundry in the opening pages of Act III. Ex. 19b i has the harmony of the *Pelléas*-extract at the same pitch, but not the same movement of parts (this harmony has also occurred earlier on the same page of *Parsifal*); b ii is complete in its resemblance (the parallel ninths sliding up a semitone) but a tone above the pitch of 19a. Kundry's words which immediately follow are of course 'Dienen,–dienen', and it is possible that this memorably simple setting should have had an effect on the Doctor's 'Faites . . . faites . . .' which comes on the third page after Ex. 19a. This similarity of word-setting (given in Ex. 20) is given additional resonance by the contextural similarity established in Ex. 19; the effect is to enhance the point made already,[2] that the weak and hesitant Kundry of *Parsifal* Act III resembles Mélisande throughout Debussy's opera, more especially the declining Mélisande of this final act.

Indeed Act V concerns itself solely with Mélisande's fading and death; the other characters gather round her bed and display their typical attitudes–Arkel grave and wise, Golaud distracted and unable to contain either his violent or his piteous emotions. The Wagnerian aspect of Mélisande's decline, apart from the connection with Kundry, is entirely *sub specie Tristan*, particularly (as later examples will show) the prelude to Act III. But before reaching her death, I would like first to follow to its end a *Tristan*esque

1. ' One would say her soul was cold for ever. ' ' Cold and stiff! This time well might I fear her dead. '
2. Ch. V Ex. 5a.

Ex. 19a   *Pelléas*, v.s., p. 270

Ex. 19b i
Parsifal, v.s., p. 220

Ex. 19b ii
Parsifal, v.s., p. 221

Ex. 20a
Parsifal, v.s., p.221

Ex. 20b
Pelléas, v.s., p. 243

vein running throughout Debussy's opera, one not so far mentioned because in as much as it forms a series of unrandom reminiscences of Wagner of the kind which lend themselves to formulation and interpretation, it escapes the danger pointed out at the beginning of this chapter. To elicit this vein it is necessary again to traverse the first four acts before finally concluding Act V; strict chronological treatment would lose it among a mass of accidental and incidental connections.

Debussy has already used the opening harmonies of *Tristan*; a typical example was Ex. 13c of Chapter II, where he made a strikingly direct recreation of the instrumental sonority and spacing, as well as the harmony, to accompany the Damozel's weeping. Ex. 21a requotes the relevant part of this for convenience; Ex. 21b gives the very similar phrase for a very similar situation, the moment in Act II scene ii of *Pelléas* when Mélisande suddenly begins to cry. It is immediately apparent that, whereas the quotation from *La Damoiselle* amounts to a quotation from *Tristan* too, the later passage assimilates the same harmonies in an altogether more elliptical way. It is simple to hear that this is so,

121

Ex. 21a   *La Damoiselle Elue*, v.s., p. 27
(For relationship to *Tristan*, see II, Ex. 13)

Ex. 21b   *Pelléas*, v.s., p. 82

but awkward to explain how. This example however is a crucial
one since, in as much as it makes a compromise between the
direct *Tristan*-recreation of the *Damoiselle*-passage and the more
subtly digested examples in *Pelléas* now to be considered, the
understanding of these will depend upon the unravelling of this.
But before Ex. 21 can be fully understood, various other passages

Ex. 22a   *Tristan*

Bars: 2   3   4   5   6

Ex. 22b   *Pelléas*, v.s., pp. 187-8   (voices parts omitted)

have to be considered. Ex. 22b is another that hovers between quotation and disguise. 22a gives, again, the opening harmonies of *Tristan*; 22b shows how Debussy has ornamented and extended them, at the same pitch but in a variety of different octaves, as Yniold cries to his father to let him down, at the end of Act III. The first two bars oscillate the first two chords of *Tristan*, but with the passing-notes in the wrong places—A# (no A♮) with F♮ bass, and B with D# 'alto'—the resemblance in sound is closest in the third and fourth bars where there is no distraction from the melodic line of the first two. The seventh bar of the *Pelléas*-extract corresponds to Wagner's bar 6; then Debussy has five bars (8-12) entirely on G# and D, this tritone being the one common between the second chord of the opening *Tristan*-statement, and the 'Tristan-chord' itself as, up a minor third, it opens the second statement (see 22a). So we hear the succeeding four bars of the

123

Debussy (22b bars 13-16) *just as if* they were harmonized as in the opening *Tristan*-statement—these four bars in fact provide the melody of 22a bars 2-3, while the first six bars provide its harmony.

Ex. 23   Opening of *Tristan* written as 7ths and 9ths (cf. Ex. 22a)

Debussy often obligingly facilitates comparison with his Wagnerian sources by using them at their original pitch. Ex. 23 shows how the opening of *Tristan* can be seen as a series of parallel sevenths. In the light of this we may return now to Ex. 21b and see that it is using in enharmonic guise exactly the same notes as the first chords of the first two *Tristan*-phrases; while in the light of Ex. 22 we see how it is better to understand its second chord as a transcription (exact) of the first chord of Wagner's second phrase rather than a version (altered) of the second chord of his first phrase (though indeed they do have three notes in common). Considered as 'aggregates of pitches' the Debussy of 21b is identical with the Wagner of the opening of *Tristan*—they could, so to speak, both have been constructed from the note-row of Berg's *Lyric Suite*. What makes the difference is of course the spacing of the chords and the harmonic movement that the spacing produces. Both of Debussy's *images sonores* of a woman's weeping, however direct the reference to Wagner in the earliest and oblique in the latest (Ex. 21a and b), have in common a feature that immediately makes them unWagnerian; this is their return to their initial chord (the *Tristan*-chord in its original position, not telescoped into a seventh). Wagner's use of these two chords in *Tristan* is such that the first opens up harmonic yearnings which the second extends rather than defines, leaving the listener doubly desiring a resolution. Debussy's patterns, both for the Damozel's tears and Mélisande's, contain the second, expanding, chord between two soundings of the first; thus the discontent of this first chord circumscribes the more intense expectation produced by the second—a vivid musical image of the narcissism of the Pre-Raphaelite Damozel no less than the Nabi Mélisande.

The implications of the word 'patterns' for describing Debussy's harmony are intentional. Wagner's usage depends for its expressive power, perhaps nowhere better felt in the whole range of music than here, upon our expectation of a resolution which is then denied; in Debussy's hands, these chords, as this recoil of the phrase upon itself shows, have become detached from their highly-charged grammatical connotations; they can now be manipulated and positioned according to aural predilection rather than tonal function. In these two 'compromise' examples where the relationship to the original is still clear, it might be said that the expressive *frisson* they give can be attributed to the sense of a shadowy remnant, behind the superficial linguistic dislocation, of the expressive force of the original's harmonic pull. This formulation, which has been the explicit or implicit drift of my previous analyses, provides the key to another kind of influence of Wagner upon Debussy; the glancing, disembodied usage of certain chords which, charged in the original with both grammatical and emotional meaning, have in their new context a complexity of ambiguous reference quite out of proportion to their intrinsic significance or even interest.

These examples are much less specific than 21 and 22; nonetheless they are here not because they can be discerned with a minutely-searching eye, but because the ear singles them out so surely from their context. Ex. 24 is a collection of straightforward uses in *Pelléas* of the *Tristan*-chord, 'demythologized' (in the manner described above) of the harmonic and expressive connotations it carries in Wagner. 24a shows three *Tristan* chords rising parallel a minor third apart, thus reproducing twice the relationship between the initial chords of the first two phrases of *Tristan*. 24b shows an extended use of a chord with (apart from passing-notes) the same pitches—F, E♭ = D#, C♭ = B, A♭ = G#—as the first chord of Wagner's opera. Hardly worth detailing, were it not for the fact that Debussy in the pages preceding this seems to have made almost a fetish of these same four notes in all kinds of positions—they predominate at the end of the previous scene (v.s. p. 155 four times, p. 156 twice) then begin in this next scene in the first bar of p. 162. 24c shows the same four notes, meaning the same chord, in a completely different context—24d the same again, with a touch of Amfortas in the descending major thirds. A further context for the same chord at the same pitch was seen in Ex. 21b; the same pitch-relationship in a different transposition

Ex. 24a   *Pelléas*, v.s., p. 70

Ex. 24b   *Pelléas*, v.s., pp. 168-9   (voice part omitted)

Ex. 24c   *Pelléas*, v.s., pp. 242-3

Ex. 24d
Pelléas, v.s., p. 255

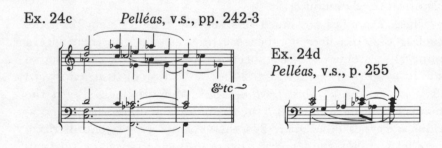

Ex. 24e   *Pelléas*, v.s., p. 219   (text omitted)

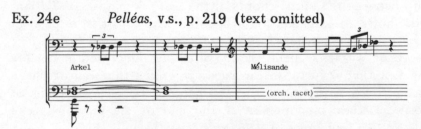

Arkel

Mélisande

(orch. tacet)

Ex. 24f   *Pelléas*, v.s., pp. 82-3   (voice parts omitted)

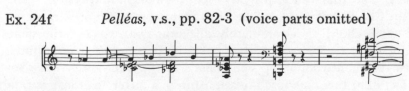

is given in 24e, while 24f gives five instances of the chord, the last two being the same as each other, and the first two being at the familiar A♭ C♭ E♭ F pitch.

The examples grouped together under 25 are of a slightly different kind, where *Tristan*-harmony gives way to *Pelléas*tique in the same progression. Thus 25a shows the *Tristan*-chord resolving into a major ninth in a way Wagner would never have permitted, and 25b answers to the same description, but is an entirely different major ninth—these two instances use the *Tristan*-chord at the same F-bassed pitch that by now is customary. Next, a passage already used earlier in this chapter (Ex. 5a) for its rhythmic resemblance to some of Kundry's music. Harmonically it is characteristically Debussyan, made out of only two chords, in four positions, each time a tone lower than the last, so that the whole phrase is circumscribed within a tritone. Ex. 25c i quotes it

Ex. 25a   *Pelléas*, v.s., p. 6

Ex. 25b   *Pelléas*, v.s., p. 218

Ex. 25c i   *Pelléas*, v.s., p. 17

Ex. 25c ii

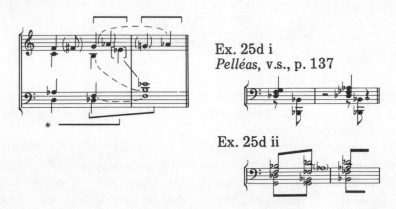

Ex. 25d i
Pelléas, v.s., p. 137

Ex. 25d ii

Ex. 25e   *Pelléas*, v.s., p. 204

again, marking the first chord of each position*—they are in fact the *Tristan*-chord; the relation of the second chord of each position both to the second chord of the initial *Tristan*-phrase and to the first chord of the second *Tristan*-phrase is indicated in c ii. Thus what at first sight seems so strikingly of its composer, yields a veiled but nonetheless direct access to the ubiquitous original. The same happens in Ex. 25d i, another phrase which (as Ex. 12a) has already been discussed under its *Parsifal*-aspect. Again it can now be subsumed under a *Tristan*-reference (25d ii) with the same simultaneous reference in its second chord to the third as well as the second harmony of *Tristan* as found in 25c. Finally, another instance of a *Tristan*-usage that slips into harmony that Wagner could not have written—in this case (25e) the sort of grave French saccharine (if the phrase can be permitted) that Debussy particularly associates with Arkel.

These eleven examples from *Pelléas* have of course been short.

of text and context simply to facilitate exposition; text and context must now be provided. 24a comes when the 'Russian' (i.e. non-Wagnerian) freshness of the garden scene[1] is nearly over. Mélisande has dropped Golaud's ring; a feeling of unease dispels the pastoral gaiety—'No, no, we'll never find it again, we'll never find any other, either . . . '. The contexts for the use of the F C♭ E♭ A♭ chord mentioned under 24b are as follows:—pp. 155-6; again a scene[2] of freshness, midday striking, the smell of newly-watered roses, the children bathing, is overshadowed by a sudden check, this time from Golaud in person—'Apropos de Mélisande . . .' and his warning to Pelléas to leave off playing childish games; in the scene following, Golaud inciting Yniold to spy upon Pelléas and Mélisande; and the example quoted, to which he cries 'Ah! misère de ma vie! . . . Je suis ici comme un aveugle qui cherche son trésor au fond de l'ocean!'[3] The changed context of 24c and d is the love-scene[4] —to c Pelléas sings that he must always be going away, and Mélisande, 'why do you always say you're going away?' But these are the shy preliminaries—24d accompanies Mélisande's wanly ambiguous statement of her 'full' love, 'I am happy, but sad . . . '. Arkel and Mélisande speak the words omitted in 24e, as Golaud's insane passion subsides—'Qu'a-t-il donc? Il est ivre?' 'Non, non, mais il ne m'aime plus . . . .'[5] 25f is in fact the continuation of the image of Mélisande's weeping given in Ex. 21b. The dialogue these chords accompany is worth quoting in full:—

Golaud	Pourquoi pleures-tu tout à coup?
Mélisande	Je suis . . . je suis malade ici . . .
Golaud	Tu es malade? Qu'as-tu donc, qu'as tu donc, Mélisande?
Mélisande	Je ne sais pas . . . Je suis malade ici.[6]

1. II i.

2. III iii.

3. ' Ah my wretched life! Here I'm like a blind man searching treasure in the depth of the ocean! '

4. IV iv.

5. ' What is it? is he drunk? ' ' No . . . he no longer loves me . . . ' (IV ii).

6. G. Why do you cry?
   M. I . . . am ill here . . .
   G. Ill? What is it then, Mélisande?
   M. I don't know . . . I am ill here. (II ii).

The contexts of Ex.25 are as follows: a is from the very first scene, where Golaud asks Mélisande why she's crying there, all alone. 25b comes just before 24e; suddenly calm, Golaud excuses himself before his trembling wife as best he can—'I am too old—and besides, I don't make a spy'. Back to the first scene for c; he explains to the unknown girl how he has lost himself following a boar. She already knows his name, has remarked that his hair and beard turn grey, has exclaimed that he is a giant; and this account of his hunting gives these physical attributes a passing substantiality. Ex. 25d i comes just at the moment in the tower-scene when ecstasy definitely gives way to fear — 'laisse-moi! laisse-moi relever la tête . . . j'entends un bruit de pas . . . Laisse-moi!'[1] — Mélisande realizing that Golaud has overheard Pelléas's rapturous hymn to her hair. Finally, the context of 25e is given by Arkel's words . . . 'to believe still in the freshness of life, and keep off for a moment the threat of death'—*Tristan*-chord; then the dry-sweet harmony of 'As-tu peur de mes vieilles lèvres?'[2]

Ex. 21b, which provided one of the fullest specimens of a near-*Tristan* usage, illustrated Mélisande's weeping at her constriction in the castle, and its unconcealed implication is her sense of oppression by Golaud. Ex. 22b, the other passage very close to the *Tristan*-original, accompanied the terror inspired by Golaud in his small son—'Oh, je vais crier . . . Laissez-moi descendre! laissez-moi descendre!'[3] What these two direct instances, and all the small instances gathered up as Ex. 24 and 25 have in common, are connotations (in varying degrees and combinations) of guilt, fear, oppression, constriction, and thraldom. Of this total of thirteen, all but three are concerned with Golaud as a man who embodies these qualities in himself, and is the cause of them in others—his wife, his half-brother, his child. His words already indicated under Ex. 24b might well serve as the motto for the whole situation that these examples uncover—'Ah! misère de ma vie!' The drama unfolds at every point through the action upon the passive characters of Golaud's dynamic pressure, his jealousy, possessiveness, spying, violence, his role as one who delivers warnings, and

1. ' Let me go! Let me lift my head! I hear footsteps! Let me go! ' (III i)
2. ' Are you afraid of my old lips? ' (IV ii)
3. ' Oh, I shall scream . . . let me down, let me down! '

interrupts a grandparent with his granddaughter-in-law (IV ii) as easily as the meetings of this same woman with her lover. These examples provide evidence to substantiate a declaration that Debussy, to focus by musical means this malign activity of Golaud, uses harmony based nearly or at a remove on the opening progressions of *Tristan*; and just as Golaud's activity is in the strongest contrast to his flaccid surroundings, so these chords, isolated from the tonal and expressive function they always preserve in Wagner, stand out in marked distinction from the pale level of the typical harmony—pentatonic, wholetone, simply diatonic, chords in parallel movement—of *Pelléas*. The image in Debussy's correspondence and journalistic writings of the wretched listener held captive to the spell of Wagner receives unexpectedly literal confirmation in these usages in *Pelléas*, where the *Tristan*-progressions, invented by Wagner to convey enthrallment of an extremely different kind, are employed by Debussy to circumscribe and colour everything in his drama repressive, inhibitory, harsh, and claustrophobic.

Elucidation of a theme like this necessarily wreaks havoc with Debussy's opera as a chronological sequence of events and music. It is time to return to, and conclude, the discussion of *Pelléas* Act V. The doctor says at the beginning that a bird would not die of such a slight wound as Golaud has given her physically; and that Mélisande is harrassed towards her death partly by the uncontainable anxiety and ferocity of Golaud's enquiries later in the act will not be denied. However the main cause seems simply to be her own ever-readiness for extinction, and as she declines, the *Tristan*-vein in Debussy's opera leaves the opening of Act I and settles decisively for the opening of Act III. Ex. 26a, the theme of Mélisande in decline, clearly recollects in its melodic and harmonic character the theme which, first appearing in the prelude to Act III, is later associated in Tristan's wandering mind with the healing arts of Isolde—26b. The similarities lie in the tempo and movement, the syncopations and sequences in the construction of the melody, their gentle poignant declivity, and the harmonization in shifting thirds. This first occurrence of the *Tristan* passage comes, as the Debussy does, to an unfulfilled close; ten bars later Wagner repeats the whole passage, transposed up a fourth, with instrumentation now also comparable to Debussy's—the melody shared between

Ex. 26a   *Pelléas*, m.s., pp. 371-2 (voice part omitted)

Ex. 26b   *Tristan*, m.s., pp. 718-19

solo clarinet, then oboe, then horn, doubled always by a single
viola-player, the descending thirds on *tutte viole* doubled by a
single clarinet and bassoon. Note also the expressive performing
instructions in both languages; *gedehnt, sehr weich, ausdrucksvoll
—triste et doucement expressif.*[1] The difference in character be-

1. drawn out, very soft, full of feeling—sad and softly expressive.

tween the two passages is customary—that Wagner's invention is intense in its poignancy; after it Debussy's version seems wan. Its second bar varies its first, the fourth the third, and the result is less sharply-defined, more arabesque-like in its oscillation around the same notes. Wagner produces a musical symbol of sickness and longing for healing; Debussy renders the pathos of the illness itself, and the words that Mélisande sings to this phrase—'Pourquoi demandez-vous cela? Je n'ai jamais été mieux pourtant . . .'[1] show how close to tear-jerking her appeal can come.

The moment is never expressed, and we apprehend her death, as the characters on the stage do, when the serving-women suddenly kneel. Arkel wishes to make sure—'I saw nothing'—the descending thirds of Ex. 26a recur, with no melody to support, only the tolling of a harp and a bell. The Doctor answers him, and the thirds now rise as Arkel acknowledges the accomplished fact. Ex. 27a gives them and 27b the passage in the prelude to *Tristan* Act III which they clearly echo. The moves in 27a are all the

Ex. 27a   *Pelléas,* m.s., p. 106 (voice part omitted)

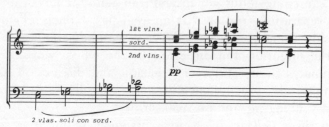

Ex. 27b   *Tristan,* Act III, bars 6-10

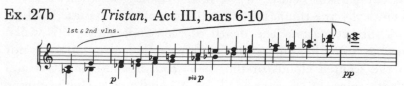

same—a major third at a minor third's distance; so that this pattern repeats itself at the octave every four notes. 27b repeats itself at the octave every six notes, all six steps are different, and not one of them is a major third to a major third at a minor third's distance. Nevertheless the resemblance is plain—it is a matter of the

1. ' Why do you ask? But I have never felt better. . . '

sounding of false relations, and to this generalized similarity the stricter resemblances of musical image (a long slow phrase for strings in two parts rising evenly into an empty empyrean) give place. Thus the death of Mélisande can be seen, in the light of the completed train of *Tristan*-references in *Pelléas*, to be the anti-affirmation of sheer emptiness. 'Öd' und leer'. These words[1] (heard to a varied repetition of 27b) have already been cited[2] in the discussion of a previous reference in *Pelléas* to the same musical phrase, the passage in Act II scene ii where Golaud talked of Mélisande's separation from the life of the castle, and asked her the question which contains the key-word of the whole opera—'Fait-il trop triste ici?'[3] The example here bears a still closer resemblance to the original, and it would be worthwhile to attempt to say fully what this resemblance implies. Pelléas died of his sword-thrust; Tristan after his sword thrust lingers on, broken and listless; Mélisande lingers listlessly on, and, listless as ever, dies; Tristan, racked with ecstatic frenzy, expires as he sees his beloved once more. But now Isolde by sheer exaltation induces in herself and the audience the feeling that his death was immaterial; a fulfilment can come about which will transcend the physicality of death and separation—and as this apotheosis, at once religiously and childishly transfiguring, is achieved, we understand that this has been the intention and direction of the whole work; everything culminates in it, and every tension and distinction it has raised, dramatically, psychologically, and musically, is resolved in dramatic, psychological, and musical terms.

In comparison *Pelléas*, by a nice instance of imitative form, has musically the thinness and emptiness of the essential nihilism of its subject-matter. The death of Mélisande shows this well—listless as ever, her music arises, thins out, and evaporates, not into the scented clouds of the *Liebestod,* but into the 'Öd' und leer' dreariness of the inner and outer condition at the beginning of *Tristan* Act III. Nothing is resolved, and it is an open question as to whether anything has even happened; the final pages of *Pelléas* are an elegy, 'mild und leise' indeed but not in the way that Isolde means; and after Arkel's assertion of the ultimate

1. *Tristan* m.s. p. 725.
2. See Ch. V Ex. 6 and discussion of it in the text.
3. 'Is it too sad here?'

passive fatalism ('C'est au tour de la pauvre petite'[1]) the music sweetly drains away to almost nothing.

And in this nothingness lies (though it is more in the nature of a metaphysical speculation than these concrete examples I have just been discussing) the final *Tristan*-connection in *Pelléas*. The *Tristan*-progression originated as a breath, the breath, as Wagner said, that 'blurs the clarity of the heavens . . . grows, condenses, and solidifies, until finally the whole world confronts me in its impenetrable bulk'. Debussy reverses this process; he liquifies, dissolves, and diminishes, until the impenetrable bulk of the *Tristan*-world vanishes into the empty nothingness from which it had been summoned. And *Pelléas* has its 'nothingness-motif' – a single tone. As a part of every other motif, or merely an intervallic oscillation, it is omnipresent; it permeates the loose-knit texture more thoroughly than the Welt-Atem or *Tristan*-progression does Wagner's essentially symphonic score – without, however, binding it together. It is in fact the embodiment of the whole disintegratory, anti-matter emptiness which the work, by its means, consists of as well as expresses. The richness of Wagner's score is already implicit in the progression of the *Welt-Atem;* the *Welt-Atem* is pregnant with the abundance and profusion of the accomplished work. By contrast the parsimony of means in Debussy's fully-achieved work implies the possibility of a reduction to the central minimum, the nothingness of a single tone. So this final point summarizes my general tendency in these chapters on *Pelléas*: in his opera, Debussy deals with a *Tristan*-like situation, that his treatment is saturated with echoes and reminiscences both of *Tristan* and other music of Wagner, but so great is the difference of culture, tradition, personality, expressive intention and artistic manners, that every indication of indebtedness, while confirming at once the strength of the influence, yet shows the indebted work negative, sour, hostile, indeed antithetical, towards both the musical substance and the psychologico-dramatic meaning of its original. And the reason for this sourness is of course that, in spite of the immense importance of Wagner's influence upon *Pelléas*, there is another side to Debussy's opera that shows the positive aspect of his conscious hostility to Wagner.

---

1. 'Now it's the little one's turn' (Mélisande's daughter).

4. *Debussy and Mussorgsky*

Consideration of the larger rather than the local aspects of Debussy's opera touches upon a paradox—that it is precisely in his employment of Wagnerian leitmotifs in *Pelléas* that Debussy stands furthest from his original.

Obvious exceptions leap to mind. Golaud introduces himself— 'Je suis le prince Golaud, le petit-fils d'Arkel le vieux roi d'Allemonde'—his motif and Arkel's accompany the words with a direct Wagnerian patness surprising in the composer who mocked the 'visiting-card' promptitude of the leitmotif system, and who wrote 'the pretence that a certain series of chords represents such a feeling and a certain phrase such a character, is an unexpected game of anthropometry'. There are other directly nominative leitmotifs in *Pelléas*, and in fact their function is so simply referential that Debussy's practice can just about be reconciled to his verbal attitude, for he never attempts motivic symbolization, only once does he follow Wagner's pictorialism[1], and only one of his leitmotifs is an 'abstraction'—the 'nothing-ness-theme' already discussed—and here comparison with the Tarnhelm will show at once that even in dealing with a nothing-ness, Wagner is thematically focused and concrete.

But of leitmotivic composition as a technique for writing an opera Debussy shows not a trace. In Chapter III I discussed Wagner's operatic practice, how the orchestra becomes the central protagonist, and the drama achieves its fullest expression in the music, so much so that the music becomes the content of the drama.[2] The means whereby he achieved the formal coherence that holds this unprecedented length and explicitness together, is of course the leitmotivic-developmental-symphonic style of musical construction. When the hacks wrote after the première of *Pelléas* that 'Debussy has arrived at the greatest negation of every doctrine . . . disowns melody . . . despises the symphony with all its resources . . .'[3] they were not so much inaccurate as merely Philistine. The structure of Wagner's massive forms is thematically and symphonically developmental, in the rich mainstream of the

1. The ' gold shining under the water ' in I i; see m.s. pp. 12 and 16.

2. See pp. 52 - 4.

3. See p. 55.

Austro-German harmonic and contrapuntal tradition. The leit-motifs that form his basic material are at once sharply defined and highly characterized in themselves, and at the same time immensely susceptible to expansion, transformation, development and combination, in an endless variety of ways. Wagner's account (my italics) of his thematic process, and what he intends it to achieve, points the contrast as clearly as possible:—

> You have only to examine the score more closely, to follow the musical motifs which, from the beginning of the Act to Tristan's death, restlessly *appear, develop, combine, separate, blend again, grow, abate, finally struggle, embrace, and inter-twine;* and then you must realize that these motifs . . . portray an emotional life, alternating between the utmost sensuality and the most firmly resolute longing for death . . . which was only capable of fulfilment here through instrumental combinations such as purely orchestral composers would hardly feel called upon to employ.

Compare this with Debussy's professed anti-symphonism in his opera, and the way in which, unprofessed, his motifs not only contribute nothing to the overall form, but are hardly, even as they stand, articulated into thematic definition. In *Pelléas* every motif shares the same intervals with every other; they can be fragmented into accompaniment or ostinato; every ostinato or accompaniment can emerge as a motif; and the harmony every-where consists of these same intervals superimposed into chords. The result is a parody and a negation of the Wagnerian achievement —either everything, or nothing, is happening at any particular moment.

The large-scale corollary of this is that there is no 'architecture' in *Pelléas;* here again the Philistine view—'Wagner had in him by instinct what Debussy never had' etc[1]—is strictly speaking hardly incorrect. This view, however, misses the very special feli-city of *Pelléas*, the way in which the turn of the speech, a passing reference, an undefined feeling or mood, immediately impresses itself upon the local expression. The music in *Pelléas* actually *reacts* to the words rather than, as in Wagner, being the expression and embodiment of them. There is surely no question that for his chosen *parlando* convention Debussy's formal instinct is exactly what is needed—the delicacy of his response to the perpetually

1. See the quotation from Ernest Newman, p. 55.

changing local situation produces a 'momentary-form' of exquisite flexibility, narrowly poised between impulsiveness and mannerism. The overall form is made up of the simple sequence of these momentary solutions; and in this larger form, though it is not so much logical as sensitively and precisely improvised, there is neither sprawling nor constraint. Within its deliberately thin, asymmetrical and unexuberant style, every element is naturally and consummately realized.

The art of this 'instinctive' construction Debussy of course learnt from Mussorgsky; and it is clear that whenever this name is mentioned, quite different criteria, both stylistic, and intentional and cultural in the widest sense, are evoked from Wagner's. 'I explore human speech; thus I arrive at the melody created by this kind of speech, arrive at the embodiment of recitative in melody . . .'—so speaks Mussorgsky, and thus Debussy interprets him—'No one has given utterance to the best within us in terms more gentle or profound: he is unique, and will remain so, because his art is spontaneous and free from arid formulas. Never has a more refined sensibility been conveyed by such simple means . . .' and now follow the words already quoted,[1] which create a touch-stone for Debussy's own ideal of freedom in construction—'nor is there ever a question of any particular form . . . it depends on and is made up of successive minute touches mysteriously linked together by means of an instinctive clairvoyance.'

This ideal of Debussy's art comes under the Wagnerian aegis not at all. But of that species of influence nicely put in an aphorism of Lichtenberg ('To do just the opposite is also a form of imitation and the definitions of imitation ought by rights to include both') the Debussy-Wagner relation, in the matter of musical form and its expressive function, is a perfect example. However as I have shown, the detailed workings, the specific gravity of the musical texture of *Pelléas* are suffused with Wagnerian influence in the more usual sense—though only usual in comparison to Lichtenberg's kind, to be sure.

It is important, in concluding these chapters on *Pelléas* under its general and particular Wagnerian aspects, to insist finally upon the vital presence of Mussorgsky in its realization; not only in terms of a 'natural' parlando and a spontaneous 'anti-musical'

1. See p. 17.

form, but also in the heart of the musical substance, in melody and rhythm and harmony. Not least, in characterization; Pelléas and Mélisande, as well as the child Yniold, have learnt their presence and delivery from *The Nursery* ('shadowy sensations of trembling anxiety which move and wring the heart'), while Golaud's self-projection is obviously closer to Boris than, say, Wotan; and all the vocal portions of Debussy's opera (that is, all of it except the interludes) *sound* more like Mussorgsky than ever they do Wagner. Mussorgsky is the direct influence which can at once be apprehended and appraised; Wagner's is wayward, secretive, undemonstrative, and can only be shown in this circuitous way.

The influences from Mussorgsky and Wagner that go into the making of *Pelléas* can be distinguished like this. Mussorgsky gives Debussy the language of lyricism and freshness—the fountain scene that opens Act II and the scene of Pelléas with Mélisande's hair that opens Act III, are the particular instances. The harmonic feel of the fountain-scene is quite different from anything that has been heard in the first act, while the chaste raptures of the *chevelure* scene represent, with the song of that name, the central and most beautiful example in Debussy's output of the Russian-inspired element. It is as if neither gaiety and innocence on the one hand, nor on the other passion however grave and muted, could be rendered by Debussy with any elements of Wagnerian vocabulary.

This 'Russian' and more specifically 'Mussorgskian' ambience is perpetually constricted by the gloomy castle, the mile upon mile of forests where one never sees the sun, the sullen jealousy of Golaud, and the general sadness and emptiness of things. Debussy renders this partly by the vein of *Tristan*-derivations discussed in section 3 of this chapter. It is the shadowy presence of Wagner's chromaticism that gives the different harmonic feel of those pages in *Pelléas* which express oppression and repression. Most of the more random Wagnerian echoes detailed in section 2, including the important *Götterdämmerung*-strain, also deal with the gloomy or violent aspects, as associated particularly with Golaud.

These emotions, together with all the other emotions in the opera, remain largely latent, and it is the orchestral interludes, some of them afterthoughts, which add stature and weight to *Pelléas*, giving voice to feelings which the characters, and the music that so faithfully follows the characters' speech, can hardly utter. And for this music that makes explicit the meaning as well as the experience, Debussy has had recourse above all to *Parsifal*.

By itself such an equation of Mussorgsky with freshness and spontaneity, *Tristan*-harmony with dumb constraint and thraldom, and *Parsifal* with the possibility of bodying forth the thraldom and constraint into overt expression, is large, bold and crude. But this formulation is the one towards which the wealth of the musical evidence, as well as the corroboratory detail, seems to tend; and, once it has been stated, appears to endorse some more general apprehensions about Debussy's opera. For *Pelléas*, compared with the exuberance and richness of earlier works such as the Baudelaire songs or *L'après-midi*, has become wan and thin. Just as this change is plainly deliberate—the self-restriction of a supreme stylist—so these adjectives are less pejorative than descriptive. Still, it is possible to feel that to achieve the perfection of wanness and thinness is less exalted a goal than the achievement of richness and bloom. It hardly requires a full-scale comparison with Wagner to point out that *Pelléas et Mélisande* shows a certain impoverishment. Debussy's ostensible denial of Wagner in *Pelléas* leads to a situation where, in Rolland's words, his 'distaste for exaggerated words and sentiments results in what is like a fear of showing the feelings at all even when they are most deeply stirred'. His denial of Wagner is a denial of himself—the attrition and emptiness he expresses is actually imitated in the restraint and servility of his music, the result of its imitating Wagner by doing the opposite. Wagner's high richness of matter and manner, and Mussorgsky's lowly credo of life not art, even at the cost of musical coherence and, sometimes, musical interest; these are strong positions held with some vehemence, consistency, and success. As artistic attitudes they are as different as could be conceived within the conventions and possibilities of those decades (the 1870s and 80s) during which their creative output overlapped. Debussy in his opera has failed to achieve a synthesis of opposites that perhaps could never have been reconciled; in addition his unresolved ambiguity towards Wagner is manifested by the extraordinary fashion in which, in a Mussorgskian prosody-opera, the Wagner of *Tristan* is used surreptitiously to colour one aspect of his subject matter, and the Wagner of *Parsifal* is used overtly (though no doubt unconsciously) to give voice to the work's otherwise latent emotions. These incompatibilities and uncertainties of style reveal a serious incompatibility and uncertainty at the very heart of *Pelléas*.

In *Pelléas* the Debussy-Wagner relation is much further advanced. at once more deep-rooted and more devious, than in any of Debussy's earlier works; the presence of strong elements of Wagner in Debussy's style is more interesting and pertinent a question now than at the time of *La Damoiselle élue*. *Pelléas* links Debussy's early works to those of his maturity; but leaves a question about the extent and nature of the Wagnerian influence that remains unanswered throughout the succeeding decade or so. These are his most prolific years and in a sense his most characteristic; everything on which his fame now chiefly rests—*La Mer*, the orchestral *Images*, the greater part of the piano works—dates from this period, and the Wagner-influence (apart from the *Golliwogg's Cake Walk*) seems to be closed. It arises again when Debussy receives a commission for another work with direct access to Wagnerian subject-matter, *Le Martyre de Saint Sébastien*.

Note: *Golliwogg's Cake Walk*

Debussy's 'negative, sour, hostile'[1] feelings towards *Tristan,* receive amusing confirmation in the well-known guying of the opera's opening in the *Golliwogg's Cake Walk*, written between 1906-8.[2] The four appearances of the Sehnsuchts-motif come in two pairs, the second pair being only a slight variant of the first. As so often, the pitch is the same as in Wagner's opening; but here its character is completely changed by harmony which has no reference at all to the so sharply-memorable *Tristan*-progression. The *Tristan*-chord, however, is present in bar 2 (and thenceforth whenever this pattern comes, which is frequently), spelt in the familiar A ♭ F E♭ C♭ enharmony.

Lockspeiser quotes with approval a view which claims it Debussy's

---

1. See p. 000.
2. Mr Langham-Smith of Lancaster University tells me of an act in the *Cirque Intellectuel* where Wagner paraded on a tightrope to a medley of leitmotifs transformed into cake-walk rhythm.

intention 'to convey that the child has glimpsed some of the artificiality and pretentiousness of real life'; I think this is silly—his own word 'guffaw' is surely nearer the mark. Debussy here expresses an irritation with Wagner and a desire to belittle him, reminiscent of his verbal gibes. However it is none the less serious for being so frivolous—the direction 'avec une grande émotion' has to be obeyed, after all, if the trio of the cake-walk is to be played properly, and proper playing tends to reveal the real feeling as well as the mordant distaste.

In fact something is shown momentarily in this little piece which occurs throughout a *jeu d'esprit* that makes an obvious comparison, Chabrier's set of *Tristan-Quadrilles*; that genuine warmth can shine through mocking hilarity; that even a straight quotation from the original can be mercilessly teased, and at the same time relished for its original expressive intention. And finally, that in the Debussy as in the Chabrier *Tristan*-parodies, both mockery and near-quotation are entirely at the service of the composers' unmistakable individuality—they are real works of Chabrier and Debussy, however slight—which distinguishes them from the *Souvenirs de Bayreuth* (by Fauré and Messager) or Casella's 'à la manière de' Wagner (or his Debussy, for that matter; or his Fauré!)—anonymous parlour games, lacking any resonance of creative self-expression.

CHAPTER VII

LE MARTYRE DE SAINT SEBASTIEN

1. Background

The proposal for a collaboration between Debussy and d'Annunzio came from the poet in November 1910. Debussy's attitude was fundamentally mixed; to d'Annunzio himself he wrote of the 'feverish excitement' set up by the idea of collaboration (30th Nov. 1910) and of the 'terror' with which he foresaw 'the moment when I shall have to make up my mind to write. Will I be able to? Will I be able to find what I want?' (29 Jan 1911). He made his public utterances the occasion for unusually communicative glimpses of his feelings about religion and sincerity in works of art. And the statement that poet and musician gave to the press in answer to the censure pronounced upon their work by the Archbishop of Paris is composed in the vein of dignified self-justification customary in such announcements.

On the other hand there is Debussy's private expression of his feelings—'this proposal means nothing to me of any worth' (to his wife 3rd Dec. 1910), and his reluctance to embark upon the project, which Ida Rubinstein and Robert de Montesquiou as well as Mme Debussy had to persuade him to overcome.

The explanation of these mixed feelings is on the face of it quite simple. Debussy had undertaken for financial reasons a project that he otherwise would not have considered. 'I wrote in two months a score which in the ordinary way would have taken me a year', he told the press—to his friends he said 'two years'; to Inghelbrecht, the chorus-master of the performance, 'I am labouring like a piece-worker, with never a look back'. In the confusion of intentions surrounding Le Martyre this remark would seem to give his most honest response; the job on hand carries little or no significance for the piece-worker, but the quicker he works (especially if there is a deadline) the more he will earn.

The financial motive would account for several of the uncharacteristic features in Debussy's agreement to collaborate on *Le Martyre*. To agree to set a text he had not yet seen is already remarkable in the composer whose achievement as a writer of songs could be described as the development of an almost painful sensitivity to the words he chose to set; and surely when he did eventually receive d'Annunzio's text he must have found its fruitiness somewhat uncongenial. Again, a composer whose only previous stage-work had progressed with the slowness that accompanies the painstaking unfolding of a new style, could hardly imagine that he could complete a score of the size and scope of *Le Martyre* in a few months. Third, and perhaps more surprising still, that an artist of such a retiring and unworldly disposition should wish to be associated with the trumpery, dubious artistically and morally, of a 'sacred mystery' by d'Annunzio, the vehicle of Ida Rubinstein's ostentation and the flamboyant theatrical acumen of the impresario Astruc.

No wonder then that Debussy found his work at once a drudge and a near-impossibility, and that his apologia for it seems so strained.[1] It is easy to understand how he might have been driven to employ Caplet to assist him with the composition as well as with the orchestration[2] of this most rapidly-produced yet unspontaneous of his works. No wonder, above all, that such a high proportion of the music of *Le Martyre* is so poor in quality.

2. Plot and Subject-Matter

The manifest inadequacies in *Le Martyre* must be due, apart from the circumstantial difficulties already mentioned, to Debussy's having undertaken a work whose strongest inducement was *not* the text and the nature of its subject-matter. Of all composers he knew best the dependent balance between the limitations and the predilections of his art, and never except in this work strayed outside either. However there are aspects of the subject-matter of

1. e.g. '. . . when in the last act the saint ascends into Heaven I believe I realized all that I have felt and experienced in the thought of the Ascension. Did I succeed? It no longer matters to me ', etc.

2. See Robert Orledge's article on the extent of Caplet's collaboration in *Le Martyre*; *Musical Times* December 1974.

Le Martyre which connect it with that of *Pelléas et Mélisande* and *La Damoiselle élue.*

The story of St. Sebastian as presented by d'Annunzio and Debussy does not need detailed retelling. The scene is Imperial Rome of the third century A.D. In the 1st Mansion (as the acts are called), *La Cour des Lys,* Sébastien performs the miracle of shooting the arrow that does not fall, and takes the place of a twin pair of Christian martyrs on a fire of coals, upon which, unsinged, he performs an ecstatic dance. In the 2nd Mansion, *La Chambre magique,* Sébastien is engaged in the destruction of paganism and magic-making. He heals the virgin Erigone of the wound caused by her clutching to herself a portion of Christ's shroud, and she is converted to Christianity; the act ends with a vision of barbaric astrology transfigured by the Virgin, who sings, as Erigone dies, of her Son. In the 3rd Mansion, *Le concile des faux dieux,* Sébastien addresses the Emperor and the pagan deities; in answer to their charges against him he presents in mime the Passion of Christ. The women, overcome by his beauty, mourn him as Adonis, and the Emperor wishes to make him a god. Sébastien's insulting refusal causes the order for his execution at the hand of his own archers, and the women wail his death as they had wailed that of Christ. The 4th Mansion, *Le Laurier Blessé,* covers Sébastien's martyrdom; during his death-agony he sees a vision of *Jesus Pastor.* The act carries through without a break into the fifth Mansion, *Le Paradis,* a scene in Heaven where the newly-liberated soul of Sébastien is greeted in turn by martyrs, virgins, apostles, and angels. The work ends with a *Chorus Omnium* singing the 150th Psalm.

Thus the plot; the subject-matter is, baldly, that kind of voluptuary longing for pain that receives its expression and its quietus in redeeming the guilty from their guilt. The feeling of a desire for pain can be felt in various forms and degrees of intensity in Pelléas, Mélisande and Golaud, as well as elsewhere in Debussy's choice of song-texts, and even, in a more tenderly unconscious fashion, in the character of the Blessed Damozel. It plainly derives from the preoccupation with the same theme in *Parsifal*; indeed it is not too much to say that *Le Martyre* bears as close a relation in subject-matter to *Parsifal* as the plot of *Pelléas* does to the plot of *Tristan.*

The parallels can be drawn somewhat as follows:— Sébastien has a dual role, that of the man consumed by guilt and suffering, and that of the *Erlöser* who takes the guilt and suffering upon himself as an atonement. In the first, Sébastien is identified with Amfortas; they share a longing for pain, though Amfortas's expression of his longing is nerve-wracked while Sébastien's remains *nerveux*. The virgin Erigone in the 2nd Mansion of *Le Martyre* is a projection of this aspect of Sébastien, and possesses like Amfortas a wound that will not heal until touched by the Redeemer. The difference between Amfortas and Sébastien is that Sébastien in his other function as *Erlöser* draws the pain to himself as a martyr or scapegoat, whereas Amfortas needs the *Erlöser* to perform this office for him before his pain can be assuaged, since he can do nothing for himself.

This second and most important part of Sébastien's dual role, the *Erlöser* or Redeemer, is directly comparable to that of Parsifal. They are in this function both Christ-figures. Sébastien acts out in dance, speech, and mime the Crucifixion before being himself martyred; while Parsifal has the Christ-like capacity to take upon himself the guilt of Amfortas's carnality, and by doing so purges mankind (or the microcosm of mankind, the Grail community) of their guilt.

3. *Weaknesses of the Music*

Guilt and suffering, and their expiation by the adoption of a Christ-like role of *Erlöser*—this is by no means close to Debussy's characteristic predilections. I would say that his feeling of self-betrayal at having bound himself to such a bargain as the composition of *Le Martyre* finds expression not only in his overt reluctance to begin the project and his reiterated complaints once it was begun, but in a concealed resistance to the necessity of dealing with emotions for which his style and temperament were so ill-equipped.

What would a man do who has by contract (and in a hurry) to fulfil a task about whose emotional suitability he is uncertain and for whose expression his technique is inadequate? He would surely find a model; he would look to the work which was the consummate expression of that emotion to show him the way, or at least to afford a few hints. At its most fruitful it could give him a convention that might be renewed by being re-employed; at its least, it might yield an idiosyncratic style that could be imitated. That is what Debussy 'did' (for I am not of course describing his literal practice) when composing the sections of *Le Martyre* which deal with the emotions of guilt and suffering; *Parsifal* now stands to Debussy as a model rather than as an influence. And therefore the echoes of Wagner in *Le Martyre* have an entirely different effect from most of those in *Pelléas*. There the unconscious reminiscences focused an emotion which without them would have remained blurred and undifferentiated. They often had the force of an allusion, a reference to something profound and powerful in the original that the new creation aspired to partake of. As such they were often extraordinarily apt and telling—the original faintly gleamed behind its recreation; and it was possible to accept the permeation as something beautiful and new, in a spirit quite different from a mere totting up of sources. But in *Le Martyre* the Wagnerian echoes are often simply imitation Wagner—the trans-forming individuality that turns a culpable plagiarism into an imaginative recomposition has not functioned, compelling a com-parison between the genuine original and its inferior imitation.

This weakness is part of the whole complex of uncertainties and ineptitudes that envelop *Le Martyre* and make its music so poor. The work's other weaknesses may briefly be enumerated. It is ramshackle, suffering from the fragmentariness that defeats almost all incidental music and all melodrama; and in this case there would seem to be no means of performance to suit modern taste and conditions. In terms of Debussy's own style the music is extra-ordinarily incoherent; it represents graphically in its inconsistency the various ways in which Debussy influenced his junior contem-poraries. Puccini, Vaughan Williams, Ravel, Bartók, and Messiaen are in this work shown in their Debussyan aspect more clearly than anywhere else. But such passages as most clearly indicate the master's influence on younger composers do not necessarily show the master at his best. Finally, even within the limitation of these strictures the quality of the music is uneven—moments of a simplicity and grandeur that cannot be paralleled elsewhere in Debussy's output are juxtaposed with commonplace fanfares and absurd 'pagan hymns'; while long stretches of the music are simply empty of any significant content.

Yet for all these criticisms there are passages in *Le Martyre* which represent an important and unexpected stage in the progress of Debussy's assimilation of Wagner, and this holds true even if it is acknowledged that these passages are not distinguished in any other way. They suggest a new maturity in his relation to *Parsifal;* an attempt to include within his range all the 'sombre colours'—the subject-matter of guilt and expiation—with which he was not yet concerned in *La Damoiselle élue.*

4. The Music Itself

On the whole the relation to *Parsifal* in Debussy's output up to now has been static; the same originals have been used again and again by the same means, to achieve characteristic moods and effects. In earlier works the flower-maidens in Act II had some importance, but the relation's evident centre was the prelude and early stages of Act III, the source of most of the Wagnerian reminiscence in *Pelléas.*

But for latter-day admirers of *Parsifal* the central drama concerns itself with the 'sombre colours' of sensuality, guilt, and redemption. The figures who bear the dramatic burden are Parsifal himself, Kundry, and above all, Amfortas. The music that accompanies Amfortas—both as he sings of his torment, the wound that will never heal, and as used, vastly augmented, to carry the communal anguish of the community of the Grail, in the Act I Transformation —is the characteristic burden of the whole work, containing the psychological and musical essence of every association that clusters around the tortuous sublimity of Monsalvat. Debussy's previous references to this central core (for instance Ex. 12 of Chapter II) have ignored these associations—have in fact been for the sake purely of colour and therefore psychologically random.

Even so late as 1914 Debussy wrote of Amfortas as 'a whining shop-girl'. But already by the time of the composition of *Le Martyre* he had shown himself less defensive in his music than in his journalism. For the parts of *Le Martyre* that call for an expression of anguish show the incontrovertible influence of the

Amfortas-strain in *Parsifal*. Here Wagner is overtly a model. Elsewhere, Debussy's Wagnerian echoes are spontaneous emanations from an unconscious that in fact reveals itself on analysis to be pregnant with delicate and signifying connections. Here they are either random, as it were 'irresponsible' references, or else, on the occasions when he seems consciously to turn to Wagner for help, they are synthetic mock-*Parsifal*. It should go without saying, the composer being Debussy, that for him to imitate Wagner is unlikely to result in anything 'Wagnerian' in the conventional sense.

First a simpler example—this reference to the unforgettable chords in *Tristan* as the lovers sink onto the flowery bank— Ex. 1a—comes as a little interruption to the recitation of the twin martyrs Marcus and Marcellus in the 1st Mansion of *Le Martyre*. Just before it they sing

Frère, que sera-t-il le monde,

Allégé de tout notre amour![1]

The first two chords of Ex. 1b unfailingly evoke Tristan's flowery bank, but this reference adds nothing to the meaning of its present context, and indeed conflicts with it rather strongly.

Ex. 1a   *Tristan*, v.s., p. 214

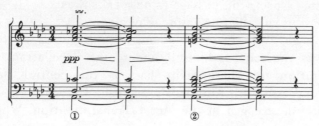

Ex. 1b   *Le Martyre*, v.s., p. 7

1. ' What will become of the world, brother, bereft of all our love? '

The association is psychologically random and musically 'irresponsible'.

The *Tristan*-citation resolves in the third and fourth bars in a way quite impossible in Wagner's harmonic idiom, and the second twin goes on to sing

J'étais plus doux que la colombe[1] (etc.)

However here there is no sense of the extension of the possibilities of Wagnerian harmony, as previously admired in analyzing *La Damoiselle élue* and the Baudelaire songs.[2] The resolution here, perhaps in accordance with the words, is cheap, almost tawdry, and can immediately be related to the decidedly stained innocence of the Vox Coelestis (v.s. pp. 42 and 45-6), and the more serious blemishes in an otherwise authentic setting, of for instance p. 4 bars 9-11, and p. 13 bars 3-4. These momentary failures of tone are of course not connected with the Wagnerian features of *Le Martyre,* but it is notable that the irresponsible reminiscence of Wagner in Ex. 1 slips at once into an harmonic vulgarity that could never have sullied the pristine progressions of *Pelléas*; and this is symptomatic of Debussy's loss of distinction throughout the work.

Ex. 2 goes to the heart of the question of Amfortas. The first extract is taken from the long orchestral section with choral interpolations (3rd Mansion no. 4) in which Sébastien mimes the Crucifixion.[3] During this passage (s)he speaks thus:

Avez-vous vu celui que j'aime, l'avez-vous vu?[4]

The first eight bars reappear identically in no. 2 of the 4th Mansion, as the saint is himself undergoing flagellation. Plainly the inspiration for these eight bars is the central *Parsifal*—sonority expressive of Amfortas's anguish. Ex. 2b gives it as it appears at full strength in the Act I Transformation. When this

---

1. ' I was gentler than the dove . . . '

2. See Chapter II, Exx. 9 and 15d.

3. 'Par ses gestes, ses attitudes, les aspects de sa face douloureuse, l'angoisse de ses paroles étouffées, le Confesseur exprime le haut drama du Fils de l'homme . . .'
   —'by his gestures and attitudes, the dolorous expression of his face, the anguish of his choked words, the Confessor expresses the high drama of the Son of Man'—d'Annunzio's direction. Confronted by this pantomime religiosity (remember this 'Christ' is a woman!) one recalls the objections early and late to *Parsifal* with its stage-spectacular celebration of Mass.

4. 'Have you seen the one I love, have you seen him?'

Ex. 2a   *Le Martyre*, v.s., p. 53
(Bars 1-8 appear identically v.s. pp. 76-7)

151

Ex. 2b   *Parsifal*, v.s., pp. 66-7
(string figure omitted)

essential difference of strength is accepted, the two extracts can
be seen to be similar in structure; the main motif of 2b lasts for
its first two bars, in bars 3 and 4 it tails off into seven bars of soft
sequential variation, then at bar 12 it is repeated a semitone
higher with only one bar of continuation before its final repetition

a minor third higher and with the most massive orchestration. Compared with this powerful asymmetry the Debussy is light-weight; and its repetitions are lower and softer rather than higher and more sonorously scored. Bars 1 and 2 correspond to the main motif (bars 1 and 2) of the Wagner; their repetition a semitone lower (bars 3 and 4) corresponds to the repetition a semitone higher in bars 12 and 13 of the Wagner; bars 5-6 are a sort of sequential diminution of the motif, and the third repetition in bars 7-8, now a ninth lower than originally, and still softer, corresponds in reverse to bars 15-16 of the Wagner, which are highest and loudest—Wagner's expression of pain rises to a climax of self-flagellation, Debussy's cringes lower and lower in self-abasement.

The immediate similarity is the effect of the descending major thirds; it is this that establishes the Wagner as Debussy's source for the emotion that characterizes the original, given by Amfortas's first words addressed some pages later to the assembled community, and sung to exactly the same phrase:—

Wehe! Wehe mir der Qual![1]

Then it is worth noting that both the Transformation music and the music of Sébastien's mime are march-like in rhythm; the one a religious procession, ceremonial, heavy and at times overwhelmingly powerful, the other plangent and throbbing, a representation (with a touch of the Hollywood religious epic) of the *via crucis*. The Wagner is at once loaded down with rhythmic and harmonic suspensions and buoyed up by a leaping figure on the strings; these in combination with the sonorous denseness of the orchestration have an effect well-rendered in Proust's description of the effects of Wagner's music . . . 'so pressing and so near, so internal, so organic, so visceral, that one would call them the resumption not so much of a musical motif as of an attack of neuralgia'. The Debussy is by contrast rhythmically simple—a uniform weary momentum. The orchestration too is light, and achieves its plangent quality by the addition and subtraction of strings to the woodwind continuum—the descending thirds passage in Wagner is always, even in *mf*, a sonorous tutti.

The end of the Debussy extract (bars 13-15—and the same rhythm continues for a further 7 bars) is a less direct reminiscence

---

1. 'Woe! Woe me the anguish!' (v.s. p.76).

of the heavy figure in the *Parsifal* Act III prelude—Ex. 2c. In tempo, one bar of this extract is equal to two bars of the Debussy, and the insistent character of the upbeat leading to a sharp *sforzando* dissonance which is immediately reduced in volume has possibly remained in Debussy's mind from this particularly fertile tract of *Parsifal*. Also the *schwer* drum-beats are a characteristic of Act III. In Ex. 2d they are tuned a tritone apart, as in the Debussy, when Gurnemanz reminds Parsifal of Christ and his Cross—a direct link in subject-matter, since it is the function of Sébastien's mime to convey to the Emperor "les douleurs du Fils de l'homme".

Ex. 2c   *Parsifal*, v.s., p. 215

Ex. 2d   *Parsifal*, v.s., p. 249

Ex. 3c comes a few bars later in the same number of *Le Martyre*—the change of mood is heralded by the saint's

Il dit alors: Mon âme est triste jusqu'a la mort.[1]

Debussy remains on familiar territory, the prelude to Act III of *Parsifal* with its incomparable rendering of spiritual attrition. The relation of this passage of *Le Martyre* to the opening of *Parsifal* Act III has exactly the same significance as it had in the interludes of *Pelléas*[2]—here the *Parsifal*-solution is even more dilute.

1. 'then he said, My soul is heavy even unto death.'
2. See Chapter V, Exx. 2 and 5.

The general aura of the Act III opening is reflected in the
Debussy, dimly as if through veil upon veil of damp muslin;
but there are two instances of a more specific resemblance. The
movement of the harmony in Ex. 3a with its characteristic
oscillation between various chromatic chords, settling down only
to move off again, seems to exert a kind of pressure on the
harmony in the Debussy example—3c—where the oscillation is
even more aimless and tenebrous. The other resemblance is
perhaps more theoretical than audible. Ex. 3b is the quintessential
chord of the *Parsifal* Act III prelude (it comes, in different
transpositions, in bars 10-11, 26-7, then 31-2 and 33-4). I have
already noted Debussy's use of this very dissonant chord in the
interlude between Act II scenes 1 and 2 of *Pelléas*.[1] The last bar
of this extract from *Le Martyre* contains the five notes of this
chord in inversion—Ex. 3d—but so dispirited and sketchy has this
music become that it is as if Debussy cannot summon the energy
to sound all the notes at once.

Ex. 3a   *Parsifal*, v.s., pp. 215-16

Ex. 3b
Chord in *Parsifal* Act III prelude (bars 10-11, 26-7, 31-4, etc)

The same music returns a few pages later in *Le Martyre* up an
octave and a semitone, with the moving bass now transferred into
an inner part—Ex. 3f. This is the background to the continuation
of the Saint's melodrama: he has now reached the shattered tomb:—

1. See Chapter V, Ex. 5f.

Ex. 3c   *Le Martyre,* v.s., pp. 54-5

'. . . pourquoi cherchez-vous parmi les morts celui qui est vivant? Or, il est la, debout. Il dit: 'Ne pleurez plus! . . .'[1] Here the seventh, now in E major, is equally noticeable, and a little suspension in bar 4 of the example presents itself as a possible remote reminiscence of the pure fool motif in *Parsifal*— Ex. 3e.

Ex. 3e   The 'Pure Fool' motif (i.e. *Parsifal,* v.s., p. 44, transposed up a semitone)

This ends the noteworthy Wagnerian references in the music of *Le Martyre.* There are further fleeting glimpses of the harmony of *Parsifal,* but nothing even so tenuously clear as Ex. 3 e and f.

---

1. '. . . why seek ye the living among the dead? Now he is there, arisen. He said, "Do not weep!" . . .'

Ex. 3f   *Le Martyre*, v.s., p. 61

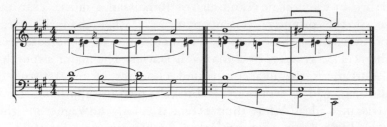

However a strong connection, albeit negatively rather than positively defined, is implied between the two works by some further
remarks of Debussy's about *Parsifal* from which I have already
quoted.

> The atmosphere is certainly religious, but why have the
> incidental children's voices such sinister harmonies? Think
> for a moment of the childlike candour that would have been
> conveyed if the spirit of Palestrina had been able to dictate
> its expression.

This criticism must be taken with one of the statements Debussy
gave to the press at the time of *Le Martyre*. Having complained
that the authentic style of religious music came to an end with the
sixteenth-century polyphonic masters, he gives his own version of
composition as a spontaneous inspiration from natural beauty, and
concludes

> I wish to write down my musical dreams in a spirit of utter
> self-detachment. I wish to sing of my interior visions with
> the naive candour of a child.

The connection thus established between the two works is of a
negative kind—Debussy finds the choral element in Act I and at the
end of Act III of *Parsifal* 'sinister' and lacking in 'childlike
candour', which can be paraphrased as meaning 'sophisticated
and artistically conscious at the expense of spontaneity and
freedom'. The truth or not of this judgement is immaterial; the
point is that Debussy's experience of what Hanslick admired in
Parsifal as 'rhythmically ordered and melodically self-sufficient
song, and multiple-voiced song at that' has stimulated him, by a
typically perverse mixture of admiration and opposition, to put
forward his own ideal of the dictation of Palestrina's spirit.
Debussy loved the polyphonic masters—his letters mention Lassus,

Palestrina and Victoria—though his love was of course a 'naive' pleasure in the archaic 'candour' of Renaissance music, akin to a love of the primitive Italian painters, rather than the ascetic appropriation of these composers' techniques that characterizes a Webern, a Stravinsky, or a Maxwell Davies. The major strength of *Le Martyre* is the unaccompanied choruses in the 1st and 5th Mansions, which represent Debussy's nearest approach to his Renaissance ideal. While their effect is totally unWagnerian, there can be little doubt that he learnt the effectiveness for stage and atmospheric purposes of these childlike strains from what he was pleased to call the 'sinister harmonies' of

ces voix d'enfants chantant dans le coupole.

5. Conclusion

The well-known story of Debussy's uncontrollable weeping at the final dress-rehearsal of *Le Martyre* tells as convincingly as any analysis that certain aspects of the work's subject-matter disturbed him more profoundly than the weak quality of the music, considered in isolation, would warrant. That *Le Martyre* is one of his weakest scores no-one surely would doubt; but nevertheless the attempt to assimilate the Amfortas-strain in *Parsifal,* unsuccessful though it is, can be taken as a sign of a deepening in Debussy's artistic nature and capacities. To the familiar psychological repertory of enervation derived from *Parsifal* Act III and voluptuous enticements and magical or angry gestures derived from Act II he now adds the burden of Act I—the agonies of carnal and spiritual guilt. An awareness that such emotions exist, rather than a direct embodiment, or rounded portrayal of them. So classically total and masterful a presentation as that of Amfortas or Kundry was out of the question for Debussy because of the nature of the work and the circumstances of its composition and anyway impossible because so alien to his culture and artistic 'manners'. But now, with the new range of experience opened to him by the assimilation in *Le Martyre* of *Parsifal* Act 1, he is ready for *Jeux;* and there, treating this new subject-matter with his own 'manners' rather than those dictated by outward pressures, he produced a coherent, if still selective, amalgam (of the highest musical quality) of the richness of psychological meaning and musical material in all three Acts of *Parsifal*.

*

If this treatment of *Le Martyre de Saint Sébastien* has been consistently to Debussy's disadvantage, this is regrettable but inevitable; he was writing 'piece-work' much too quickly and for the wrong reasons—fame, establishment, money. The musician of the most refined instinctive feeling, or rather predilection, for the texts and subjects appropriate to his gifts, has ventured 'ohn' Urlaub!'[1] out of his native territory, challenging the greatest master on one of his central themes. The outcome is this distressing work, which fails because it is at once too pretentious and too modest; ambitious when it has no resources to justify ambition, yet not content to do well what lies easily within its power.

Möge das er sühnen, dass schlecht er Gralsgebote hält![1]

---

1. See *Parsifal* v.s. p. 19.

CHAPTER VIII

JEUX

1. Scenario

The proposal for Debussy to write an original ballet came from Nijinsky and Diaghilev after the *succès de scandale* in May 1912 of Nijinsky's performance of *L'après-midi d'un faune*. The idea for the scenario was Nijinsky's own. Debussy found it at first 'idiotic' but eventually accepted it in a modified form. There is little doubt that, as with *Le Martyre*, the financial inducement played quite an important part in his agreement to write *Jeux*; but nonetheless Debussy wrote the work willingly and with astonishing speed. It is, moreover, the only one of his late orchestral and choral works (apart from *Rondes de Printemps*) for which neither an amanuensis nor an orchestrator were required.

Nor was Debussy pleased with Nijinsky's choreography, and their evident incompatibility must have contributed to the failure of the première in May 1913. The main reason, however, is a scenario which, if not 'idiotic', is of an implausibly artificial simplicity. Debussy's account in a letter to *Le Matin* of 15th May 1913 (two days after the première), gives it succinctly:

> In this scenario there is a park, a tennis court, there is the chance meeting of two girls and a young man seeking a lost ball, a nocturnal mysterious landscape, and together with this a suggestion of something sinister in the darkening shadows of night.

Nijinsky's original idea had been still more insubstantial:

> There should be no *corps de ballet,* no ensembles, no variations, no *pas de deux,* only boys and girls in flannels and rhythmic movements. A group at a certain stage was to depict a fountain, and a game of tennis was to be interrupted by the crashing of an aeroplane.

It is this initial idea—fondly dreamt up by Nijinsky as the 'plastic vindication of the man of 1913'—that Debussy had found 'idiotic and unmusical'; whereas he went on to add of the scenario in its final form,

> Elevations, turns, certain unforeseen, capricious steps of the dancers—everything calculated to bring alive rhythm in music is here.

Nijinsky's *Diary* gives a different version of the origin of the scenario. 'The story of this ballet is about three young men making love to each other', he writes, and a little later:

> I do not mind if Diaghilev says that he composed the stories of *Faun* and *Jeux* because when I created them I was under the influence of 'my life' with Diaghilev. The *Faun* is me, and *Jeux* is the life of which Diaghilev dreamed. He wanted to have two boys as lovers. He often told me so, but I refused. Diaghilev wanted to make love to two boys at the same time, and wanted these boys to make love to him. In the ballet the two girls represent the two boys and the young man is Diaghilev. I changed the characters as love between three men could not be represented on the stage. I wanted people to feel as disgusted with the idea of evil love as I did, but I could not finish the ballet. Debussy did not like the subject either, but he was paid 10,000 gold francs for this ballet and therefore had to finish it . . .

Lockspeiser's view, that 'it is doubtful whether one can trust more than a fraction of the salacious gossip which appears in [Nijinsky's] published *Diary* on the origin of his two ballets on the scores of Debussy' is surely not tenable. The point about the *Diary* is its naive candour and directness about his feelings and experiences. This transparency makes it as unlikely for Nijinsky not to tell the truth, as it is for him to indulge in 'salacious gossip'—it is not his style. It seems to me probable that this version of the origin of *Jeux* is more true than false—and anyway, once made, the suggestion (even if it were to come from a source altogether more questionable) inevitably takes root in the ambiguity surrounding the work.

So whatever the truth, these quotations from Nijinsky have certainly the effect of making more vivid Debussy's 'suggestion of something sinister in the darkening shadows of night', or as he puts it—no less vague but more unequivocal—in a letter of November 1913 to Stravinsky, 'the "horrors" that occur among these three characters'.

The full choreographic instructions of the ballet appear in the piano score thus:—

Le Rideau se lève sur le parc vide.

Une balle de tennis tombe sur la scène . . . Un jeune homme, en costume de tennis, la raquette haute, traverse la scène en bondissant . . . puis il disparaît.

Du fond, à gauche, apparaissent deux jeunes filles craintives et curieuses.

Pendant un moment, elles semblent ne chercher qu'un endroit favorable aux confidences.

Une des jeunes filles danse seule.

L'autre jeune fille danse à son tour.

Les jeunes filles s'arrêtent interloquées par un bruit de feuilles remuées . . . on aperçoit le jeune homme au fond, à gauche, qui semble se cacher . . . il les suit dans leurs mouvements, à travers les branches . . . il s'arrête en face d'elles . . .

Elles commencent par vouloir fuir . . . mais il les ramène doucement . . . et leur fait une nouvelle invitation.

Il commence à danser . . .

La première jeune fille court vers lui . . .

Ils dansent ensemble.

Il lui demande un baiser . . . elle s'échappe . . . nouvelle demande. Elle s'échappe . . . et le rejoint, consentante.

Dépit et légère jalousie de la seconde jeune fille.

Les deux autres restent dans leur amoureuse extase.

Danse ironique et moqueuse de la seconde jeune fille.

Le jeune homme a suivi cette dernière danse par curiosité d'abord, y prenant ensuite un intérêt particulier; il abandonne bientôt la première jeune fille, ne pouvant résister du désir de de danser avec l'autre . . .

'C'est ainsi que nous danserons.'

La seconde jeune fille répète la même figure, d'une manière moqueuse.

'Ne vous moquez pas de moi.'

Ils dansent ensemble . . .

Leur danse se fait plus tendre.

La jeune fille s'échappe et va se cacher derrière un bouquet d'arbres.

Disparus un moment, ils reviennent presqu' aussitôt, le jeune homme poursuivant la jeune fille.

Dans l'emportement de leur danse, ils n'ont pas remarqué l'attitude d'abord inquiète, puis chagrine, de la première jeune fille qui tenant son visage entre ses mains veut s'enfuir. Sa compagne essaie en vain de la retenir; elle ne veut rien entendre.

La seconde jeune fille réussit à la prendre dans ses bras.

Pourtant, le jeune homme intervient en écartant leurs têtes doucement.

Qu'elles regardent autour d'elles; la beauté de la nuit, la joie de la lumière, tout leur conseille de se laisser aller à leur fantaisie.

Ils dansent désormais tous les trois.

Le jeune homme, dans un geste passioné, a réuni leurs trois têtes . . . et un triple baiser les confond dans une extase.

Une balle de tennis tombe à leur pieds . . . surpris et effrayés, ils se sauvent en bondissant, et disparaissent dans le profondeurs du parc nocturne.

To listen to the music of *Jeux*, following in detail the way in which it applies itself to the illustration and enactment of this scenario, yields an immediate *answer*; a revelation of the reason

The curtain rises on an empty park. A tennis ball falls—a young man, dressed for tennis, racquet held high, leaps across the stage, then disappears. From backstage left two young girls appear, timorous and inquisitive. For a moment they seem to look for nothing but a place to exchange their secrets. One dances alone, then the other in her turn; they cease, abashed by the sound of rustling leaves. The young man, backstage left, seems to be hiding and following their movements through the branches—he stops in front of them. They want to run away but he gently leads them back and invites them to start again. He begins to dance—the first girl runs towards him—they dance together. He wants to kiss her—she escapes—he tries again—she again escapes—then yields, and joins him.

Chagrin and pique of the second girl. The others remain in their amorous pleasure, as the second girl dances with mocking irony. The young man follows this dance from the outset with interest, and soon with eagerness; he abandons the first girl, unable to resist the desire to dance with the other—'Thus do we dance'. The second girl imitates his movements mockingly—'Don't you tease me'. They dance together.

Their dance becomes more tender. She detaches herself and hides behind a clump of trees. Vanishing for a moment, they soon reappear, the young man pursuing the girl, and together they renew their dance.

Carried away, they have not noticed the anxiety growing into distress of the first girl who, face in hands, makes to flee. Her friend tries in vain to hold her—she will hear nothing.

At last the second girl succeeds in taking her in her arms. However the young man intervenes and gently separates them. The girls look around—the beauty of the night, the joy of the light, everything tells them to abandon themselves to their fancy.

From now on all three dance together. The young man in a passionate motion brings together their heads, and a triple kiss mingles them in an ecstasy.

A tennis ball falls at their feet—startled and scared they leap off, disappearing into the depths of the shadowy park.

for the score's being constructed the way it is. For Debussy has conveyed with astonishing success all the subtle variations of mood that the choreographic plot demands. But in the face of the immediate *question*—where, in so tenuous a caprice as this can be found the significance, even profundity, that should by rights be expected of a masterpiece?—this answer does not get very far.

This question, which I will return to, can be postponed for the moment by a remark of Herbert Eimert, who in the context of the mistake of looking for 'depth' in the work, eventually solves the difficulty by calling it 'a ballet whose subject is itself to a large extent the dance.' The pointlessness—absurdity even—of its ostensible subject, particularly when taken with the outstanding distinction of its musical substance, has defeated even this subtle critic; for I detect behind Eimert's remark the lingering ghost of that most banal critical commonplace of yesteryear, the 'work of art about itself'. Certainly the form-and-content difficulties of *Jeux* make this formula very tempting; it is none the less banal, as I shall hope to show.

2. *The Background to the Music*

The main indication that the music of *Parsifal* was associated for Debussy with *Jeux* is the well-known remark in a letter to André Caplet written during the composer's work on the score:

> Il faudrait trouver un orchestre 'sans pieds' pour cette musique.—Ne croyez pas que je pense à un orchestre exclusivement composé de cul-de-jattes! Non! Je pense à cette couleur orchestrale qui semble éclairée par derrière et dont il y a de si merveilleux effects dans 'Parsifal'![1]

To understand the importance of his enthusiasm for the orchestra of *Parsifal* it must be considered in the light of other remarks of Debussy about the instrumental aspect of Wagner's music. In the preamble to *M. Croche*, which must have been written specially for this collection of various articles whose publication in book

---

1. 'It is necessary for this music to discover an orchestra "without feet". Don't imagine I'm thinking of an orchestra composed entirely of cripples! No! I'm thinking of that orchestral colour which seems illuminated from behind, which you find to such marvellous effect in *Parsifal!*'

form was interrupted by the outbreak of war, the anti-dilettante makes a comparison between

> Beethoven's orchestration, which he visualized as a black-and-white formula resulting in an exquisite gradation of greys— and that of Wagner, a sort of many-coloured 'make-up' spread almost uniformly, in which, he said, he could no longer distinguish the tone of a violin from that of a trombone.

Debussy's own diaphonous orchestral style is the direct antithesis of the 'espèce de mastic multicolore' which he attributes to Wagner's orchestral writing; but this is in itself a connection—the achievement of the characteristic Debussyan orchestral sonority is its kneading of the Wagnerian putty, filling it with yeast, lightening the polychrome viscosity into a translucent shimmer. That is what Debussy means in the letter to Caplet by 'un orchestre sans pieds'; and it stands as a microcosmic epitome of the whole Wagner-Debussy relationship—what is latent and accidental in the one becomes the central interest of the other.

For Debussy must surely have excepted *Parsifal* from his strictures. I have already quoted his admiration for its orchestra 'lit from behind'; later in *M. Croche* we find the tribute to *Parsifal's* 'strength and serenity'; and my italics in the final sentence of homage—' there are *orchestral sonorities* that are unique and unexpected, noble and strong. It is one of the finest *monuments of sound* ever raised to the indestructible glory of music'—place the emphasis firmly on his own immediate concerns. And this admiration for *Parsifal*, in a context deriding its libretto[1], focuses on Wagner's achievement of a 'footless orchestra' in Debussy's favourite parts of the opera; he singles out for special praise 'the serene beauty' of the prelude to Act III and the entire Good Friday episode.

Debussy's view of the sonority of *Parsifal* corresponds with Wagner's own intention. 'His surface preoccupation', writes Ernest Newman,

> . . . was mainly with problems of harmony and orchestration, with refining his ceaselessly developing harmonic sense to ideal conformity with the spiritual poignancies of his subject, and endowing this strange new world of his with an orchestral colour and texture entirely its own. The colour, he told Cosima, he wanted to be at the furthest remove imaginable

1. See p. 20.

from the scoring of the *Ring*: it must have the softness and shimmer of silk, must be like 'cloud layers that keep separating and combining again.'[1]

Finally there is the curious remark in a letter to Stravinsky of April 1913; commending *Petrushka*, Debussy speaks of its 'orchestral infallibility, that I have found only in *Parsifal*'.

In this compliment to Stravinsky (which can hardly have afforded him much pleasure; Debussy immediately adds, 'You will understand what I mean, of course') *Parsifal* stands as the criterion of an orchestral standard; while the conclusion to be drawn from the letter to Caplet in the light of further remarks about *Parsifal,* is that it stood in his thoughts during the composition of *Jeux* as a touchstone, an almost magical embodiment of the new effects he was seeking to recreate for himself.

Debussy undoubtedly achieved his orchestral ideal in this work. Stravinsky repays the compliment 45 years later when he finds. *Jeux* 'an *orchestral* masterpiece, though I think some of the music is "trop Lalique".'[2] But in fact the connection with *Parsifal* is deeper than that of a common ideal of orchestral sonority; I would go so far as to say that *Jeux* manifests a kind of *Parsifal*-identification. Such an identification, however, though implicit in the music, is no longer brought into being by the subject-matter and its music in Wagner having a specific effect on the same things in Debussy, as had been the case hitherto. In *Jeux* nothing is direct, every influence is latent, suggested, sublimated; analysis must necessarily, in the spirit of the work, proceed 'sans rigueur', and reach its conclusions through 'nuance after nuance'.

1. *Life of Wagner*. Vol. IV, p. 581. Newman's continuation is particularly interesting in the light of Debussy's predilection, both in his article on *Parsifal* and in his music, for the prelude to Act III. Wagner ' was particularly conscious of the difficulties confronting him in the composition of the prelude to the third act. This music, he saw, called for a new harmonic weaving: the spiritual gloom and tension would have to be unbroken, yet within them there would have to be nuance after nuance. The form, again, could not be preimposed; it would have to be born out of the inner logic of the moods'. This last is exactly what Debussy praises Mussorgsky for.
2. *Conversations with Igor Stravinsky*. He amplifies this opinion somewhat in *Memories and Commentaries*.

3. *The Music*

The territory in *Parsifal* likely to exert the most immediate fascination for Debussy as a touchstone for *Jeux* is that ruled over by Klingsor and his unwilling slave Kundry—everything in Act II concerned with enticements, voluptuousness and magic. In the opening scene between Kundry and Klingsor, and in the scene following, between Parsifal and the flower-maidens, Debussy found the inspiration for his orchestral ideal.

The obvious starting-point for a comparison is the magic garden of 'teuflisch holde Frauen'. The meaning of this garden is the same as the garden in which *Jeux* is set—it is the garden of erotic dalliance and transitory earthly delight, as depicted for instance in the second book of *The Faerie Queene* and the central panel of the famous altarpiece by Bosch. The function of the flower-maidens in *Parsifal* and the two jeune filles in *Jeux* is to convey a feeling of voluptuous flirtation and enticement. In both works a delicate proliferation of arabesque is used to suggest the presence of garden and girls.

In musical terms the basic common factor in both works is the feeling of the waltz—or to be more exact, waltz in Wagner and valse in *Jeux*. The flowermaid scene in *Parsifal* is a waltz-sequence, with a long introduction in common time (v.s. pp. 126-138) characterized by an ever-shifting palpitation and flurry of harmony and rhythm. The waltz-rhythm begins when Parsifal 'springs somewhat further into the garden' (pp. 138-9), and the maidens' mood changes from pattering to caressing. On p. 146 (with a tempo indication worthy of *Jeux*) the tempo gently relaxes into the main waltz-theme, 'Komm! Holde Knabe!' The movement is graceful and rather languorous, gradually intensifying in expressive quality until the second stage (p. 160) when the maidens, now lively in rhythm, quarrel gently among themselves for Parsifal's favours. He interrupts them 'half angrily' (p. 166) and is himself spellbound by the voice of Kundry in her role as chief flower-maiden temptress, calling him by his name for the first time. Kundry dismisses the girls, who sing briefly of their regret (to the same enharmonies of the 'introduction' but now in $\frac{6}{8}$ – p. 169) before skittishly running off, leaving Parsifal to face a seduction more subtle and thoroughgoing.

To say that *Jeux* is a sequence of valses would be strictly true, since it is largely written in triple time, usually a nimble $\frac{3}{8}$; but it gives the wrong impression. Rather it is a mosaic-construction, or as Eimert calls it, a 'vegetative form', in which fragments of all kinds of valse-movement rush tantalizingly past, of which only a few are now and again taken up with any continuity. I do not aim, in discussing examples of waltz and valse rhythms, to establish overt reminiscences in *Jeux* of the flowermaiden music. Rather, the two have the same effect upon the listener; the influence, in as much as it still is an influence, has become assimilated beyond the need of citation.

Ex. 1a is the main waltz-theme for the flowermaidens, as they 'dance in a graceful childlike manner about Parsifal, caressing him gently'. 1b is a fragment of *Jeux*-valse that moves in the same half-hesitant swaying rhythm; it occurs as the jeune homme and the first girl dance together for the first time. A few bars later 'il lui demande un baiser'—Ex. 1c—and the same kind of movement, marked ' doux et caressant ', spreads itself wide in the strings —a gesture very close to the opening of Debussy's early setting of Verlaine's 'C'est l'extase langoureuse'—Ex. 1d—clearly indicating the meaning of these four bars in *Jeux*. Wagner's theme is at once extended and developed, whereas the Debussy is a momentary apparition, appearing twice, and then abandoned.

Ex. 2b is a sample of the second stage of the flower-maiden waltz-sequence—the more lively rhythm of the girls' coy jealousy. 2c shows the same motif as it appears in § after Kundry's interruption. But before these, there is a reminder (Ex. 2a) of the premonition of the magic garden offered by Gurnemanz in Act 1. The sonority these examples have in common is their use of parallel first-inversion triads (of course in this usage Ex. 2a is directly a forerunner of 1a)—one of the most conspicuous elements

Ex. 1a   *Parsifal*, m.s., p. 456

168

Ex. 1b *Jeux*, f.s., p. 42   **Ex. 1c** *Jeux*, f.s., p. 43

*marked 'doux et caressant' in pft. score

Ex. 1d   Debussy: *C'est l'extase*, opening (*Ariettes oubliées*, p. 1)

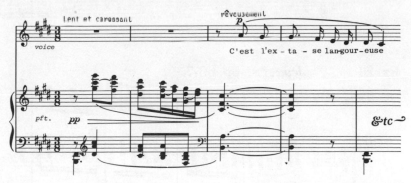

Ex. 2a   *Parsifal*, m.s., pp. 123-4

169

Ex. 2b   *Parsifal*, m.s., pp. 49⁸9-50⁰1

Ex. 2c   *Parsifal*, m.s., p. 51⁰1

Ex. 2d   *Jeux*, f.s., pp. 66-7

in the *Jeux*-sonority. Ex. 2d is chosen out of hundreds of possible examples; the woodwind and trumpets move in semiquaver parallel chords, the violins in demisemiquavers.

An intensification of this sound of parallel common-chords comes when they slip from one key to another. Ex. 3a shows an instance of this in the Wagner, strikingly reminiscent of one of the most memorable harmonic events in *Jeux* (Ex. 3b—this same passage occurs again a few pages later).

Ex. 3a   *Parsifal*, m.s., pp. $49^6 7$-$49^8 9$

(continued by Ex. 2b)

Ex. 3b   *Jeux*, f.s., p. 61

Now a different kind of waltz-movement in *Parsifal*—Ex. 4a, as the girls sing

    Und willst du uns nicht schelten,
      wir wirden dir's entgelten . . .[1]

This, again, engenders nothing in *Jeux* directly, but stands instead as a type of movement, languishing and delicious, whose effect Debussy re-creates. It is in this spirit that passages like Exx. 4b, c, and d should be understood—passages which take up the hint of voluptuousness in the Wagner, extending and subtilizing the range into an area of veiled erotic *pudeur*. Indeed they are all,

1. ' And so thou wilt not chide us
  Reward wilt find beside us. '
  I give, here and elsewhere, the Glyn translation; for all its quaintness it conveys better than a modern English version the quality of Wagner's original words.

it should be noted, emblems of escape; b—'elle s'échappe . . .';
c—'la jeune fille s'échappe et va se cacher derrière un bouquet
d'arbres . . .'; d—'la première jeune fille . . . tenant son visage entre
ses mains veut s'enfuir . . .'[1]

Ex. 4a   *Parsifal*, m.s., pp. 44^{6}7-448

Ex. 4b   *Jeux*, f.s., p. 44

The examples so far have illustrated generalities of musical-
cum-psychological rhythmic character. In considering the details of
the 'delicate proliferation of arabesque' the resemblances are
much more direct. *Jeux* is a score miraculously rich in all kinds of
ornament; and in the flowermaiden scene, though it is in com-

1. See scenario.

Ex. 4c   *Jeux*, f.s., p. 65

Ex. 4d   *Jeux*, f.s., p. 75

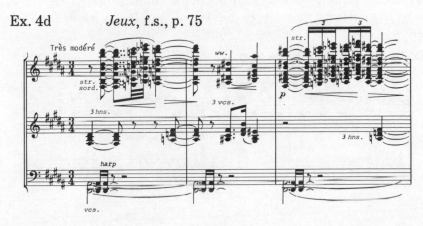

Ex. 5a   *Parsifal*, v.s., p. 149

Ex. 5b   *Jeux*, f.s. pp. 97-8

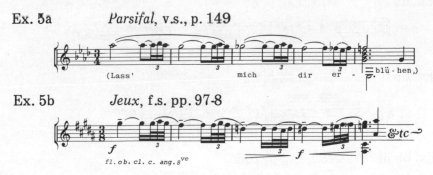

parison simple in its embellishment, may be found occasional hints
for what in *Jeux* becomes the norm. Exx. 5 and 6 demonstrate
the effect that the flowermaidens' typical arabesque figure, Ex.
5a, has upon the typical decorative motifs to be found throughout
the Debussy. Ex. 5b has a particularly direct resemblance—
especially in the way they both oscillate towards and eventually

rest upon a chord of the ninth.[1] Ex. 6a gives four bars of the
flowermaid music where the rate of variation in the ornament is
much quicker than usual in Wagner (it of course derives from Ex.
5a). Ex. 6b i-iv shows Debussy's 'vegetative' variations on this
decorative figure, at widely different points in the work. Ex. 6c
shows the elimination of the flowermaid-motif in the last few
pages of the ballet. Ex. 7 (another variant of Ex. 6a with harmony
stemming from the introduction to the waltz-sequence) is quoted
because it gives a summary in a couple of bars of the feathery
decorative effects that are to be found on almost every page of
Jeux.

Ex. 6a　　　*Parsifal*, m.s., p. 49⁶ 7

Ex. 6b i　　　*Jeux*, f.s., p. 45

Ex. 6b ii　　　*Jeux*, f.s., p. 62

Ex. 6b iii　　　*Jeux*, f.s., p. 106

1st vlns. 8ᵛᵉ above
2nd vlns. loco
vlas. tritone lower

1. Incidentally, in the piano-score of *Jeux*, transcribed by the composer, this passage is
   omitted and a completely different figuration substituted in small notes above the
   main outline which the pianist plays (see pft. score, p. 35, third stave).

Ex. 6b iv   *Jeux,* f.s., pp. 111-12

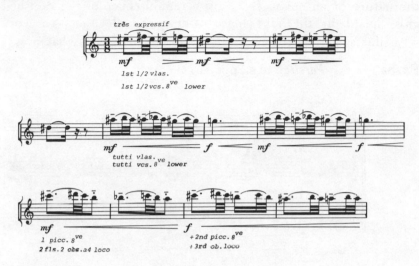

Ex. 6c   *Jeux,* f.s. pp. 113-14

Ex. 7   *Parsifal,* m.s., pp. 506-7

The last example concerned directly with the flower-maidens has the nature of an *envoi*. Ex. 8a is a reminiscence of the vanished girls, heard in the rapt hiatus before Kundry gets to work —Parsifal sings 'Ne'er saw I, never dreamed I yet, what now I

Ex. 8a   *Parsifal*, m.s., pp. 517-9

Ex. 8b   *Jeux*, f.s., p. 94

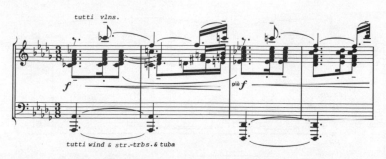

view, and e'en with dread it filleth me. And flow'rest thou too in this grove of flowers?' He begins in retrospect to understand his experience—the 'dread' shows this—and the passage is given rich significance by the *pianissimo* density of the scoring; tutti muted violins play the arabesque line, muted violas and celli support in tremolando chords, and touches of trombones and tuba give the sustained chords in bassoons and bass-clarinet a thrilling glow, particularly to the ninth in bars 5-6. A major ninth on D♭ is a striking feature of the climactic triple dance in *Jeux;* these four bars (Ex. 8b) stand out not only because this chord is so straightforward in a context of complex harmonic movement, but also because of the intensity of its expressiveness—except for piccolos, harps and lower brass the orchestral support is *tutti* (a great rarity in *Jeux*), and above it the full first and second violins play *très appuyé*. Both before (the previous 26 bars are moreover above an A♭ pedal) and after these four bars the orchestra is as usual light and full of air. But the main comparison is between Ex. 8a and a passage from the opening pages of *Jeux*, Ex. 8c. This passage from *Jeux* has just the same effect as the passage from *Parsifal*, though its use of the same elements—arabesque muted string line, here spread over five octaves, inner string tremolo, here intensified by a timpani roll, and rich wind chords—is characteristically lighter; the glow is luminous rather than sombre. The harmonies are completely different, but I have shown that the essential harmonic movement of Ex. 8a goes into Ex. 8b, a passage whose effect is not similar in the slightest. This passage of *Parsifal*, retrospective, charged with wondering delight and incipient fear, stands in Debussy's version at the beginning of *Jeux* as a foretaste

Ex. 8c   *Jeux*, f.s., p. 7

of the excitements and 'horrors' to come.

The meaning of the flowermaidens in *Parsifal* is that of a traditional *carpe diem*—

> Kannst du uns nicht Lieben und minnen
> wir welken und stirben dahinen[1]

—pleasure must be taken where and when it can, since tomorrow it will have faded. In *Jeux* the jeune homme also partakes of this meaning—the duality of Parsifal's confrontation with the maidens is not in question—the point is, of the three nymphs who dance in Debussy's garden, one is simply rather different, a flowermaid man. Whereas Parsifal is undergoing trial, and in the magic garden he is exposed to psychological danger. Pure in his foolishness, fool in his purity, he is never for a moment seriously tempted by the girls' enticements. For him only the more insidious psycho-

1. ' If thou canst not love us and cherish,
   We fading and dying must perish. '

logical temptations are real—of his latent feelings for his mother, and his uncomprehending experience of Amfortas's sensual anguish, as these fuse together, embodied in the alchemically transformed Kundry. In *Parsifal* the inmates of the magic garden are part of a progress, a particular stage in an allegory, which the hero soon sweeps aside in order that he may face the deeper issues which it raises; in *Jeux* the garden is never left—rather, all the further action still takes place within its limits.

When Debussy speaks of 'a suggestion of something sinister' and the 'horrors' in his ballet one wonders at first what, seriously, he can mean. However, once the idea dawns that *Jeux* can be seen as an assimilation of *Parsifal,* it follows that the 'horrors' of Parsifal's confrontation with Kundry might well be present in *Jeux* too. Not, of course, in the scenario.

The presence of Kundry in the *music* of *Jeux*, is incontrovertible. But in order to show this, it is necessary first to return to the opening of Act II. Kundry is here from the start what was barely hinted at in Act I, a creature driven and possessed. The dialogue showing her reluctant but total submission to Klingsor's purpose, the seduction of Parsifal, runs thus:

Kun.   Ich . . . will nicht.
Kl.   Wohl willst du, den du musst.
Kun.   Du . . . kannst mich nicht halten.
Kl.   Aber dich fassen.
Kun.   Du?
Kl.   Dein Meister.
Kun.   Aus welcher Macht?
Kl.   Ha! weil einzig an mir deine Macht nichts vermag.
Kun.   (*grell lachend*) Ha-ha! Bist du keusch?
Kl.   (*wüthend*) Was frägst du das, verfluchtes Weib?[1]

This dialogue is set by Wagner to music of an extraordinary

1. Kun.   I . . . will not.
   Kl.   You will, for you must.
   Kun.   You cannot force me.
   Kl.   But I hold you.
   Kun.   You?
   Kl.   Your master.
   Kun.   With what power?
   Kl.   Ha! Only against me will your power not avail.
   Kun.   (*laughing harshly*). Are you chaste?
   Kl.   (*furious*) Why ask me that, accursed woman?
   (v.s. pp. 114-5).

orchestral quality; the same texture recurs more briefly when
Klingsor, having cursed the fate that his unquenchable sensuality
has driven him to, cries, self-mutilated though he is, that it mocks
him still in Kundry, 'the Devil's bride'.[1] It is the orchestral
sonority here, as much as the melodic and harmonic shape of the
music, which makes these two passages a source for some of the
sonorities in *Jeux*. The general aura is of a choked sound of

Ex. 9a   *Parsifal*, m.s., p. 369

Ex. 9b   *Jeux*, f.s., p. 11

1. v.s. p. 116.

muted string tremolos and repeated chords, sharp pizzicato emphases, repeated chords on the woodwind, a shifting disturbed chromaticism in the harmony and in the deliquescent arabesque plunges on clarinet and first violins. At Klingsor's reply to Kundry's mocking final question a chord associated with her leaps out in a particularly harsh scoring—Ex. 9a. Maybe it is fanciful to suggest a connection between this and the sudden stabbing chord (Ex. 9b) in *Jeux* which announces the ballet's initial action, the bouncing tennis ball. However, the effect of these chords is remarkably similar, and this is largely due to the way they are scored; Wagner's muted horns become muted trumpets, his little shriek on clarinet and flutes becomes a shriek of grace-notes on flute and two piccolos, and while Debussy's pizzicato chord is neither explosive nor simultaneous, both these qualities are amply produced by the *sforzando* splash on the suspended cymbal.

Ex. 9c   *Jeux*, f.s., p. 12

'Are you chaste?' 'Damned woman, why ask *that*?' These questions are essentially those posed by the bouncing tennis ball, though plainly the difference in seriousness is as great as the difference in presentation! Kundry's chord is chromatically dissonant, whereas Debussy's is a simple added sixth in C major, to a flurry of whose notes (Ex. 9c) the jeune homme now appears. The manner in which only these four notes ACGE (apart from the gracenotes in the trumpets) are used in these four bars of the Debussy, is reminiscent of the passage in the flowermaiden scene as Parsifal steps further towards the girls (Ex. 9d) where only these same four notes are heard for six bars, giving a sonority very reminiscent of Debussy. The fact that it is these same four

notes again to which the bells in Acts I and III are tuned is no
doubt fortuitous!

Ex. 9d   *Parsifal*, m.s., pp. 44⁴5-44⁶7

Ex. 10a   *Parsifal*, m.s., p. 184

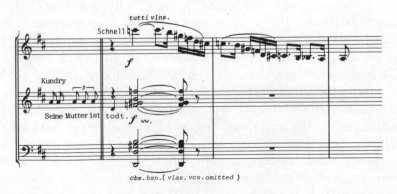

Ex. 10a is the chord and descending rushing figure by which Kundry is always characterized. In this violent form it occurs throughout the first two acts of the opera. Here, suitably enough, it accompanies her announcement that Parsifal's mother is dead;

Ex. 10b   *Parsifal*, m.s., pp. 578-80

but for her role as seductress it is capable of becoming languishing, as for example in Ex. 10b. Tenderly drooping phrases like this are a frequent element in Debussy's mature style; *Jeux* is particularly rich in them. Ex. 10c gives three little samples of these instrumental flourishes—though the chord underlying the first is rather an inversion of the *Tristan*-chord than Kundry's racking dissonance. Ex. 10d gives a more extended and direct reminder, in that the violin solo descends over two octaves as in Ex. 10a. But the difference in movement is a typical one—the Wagner rushes tempestuously down, the Debussy languidly droops in a 'fatigue amoureuse'. Finally Ex. 10e is a further version of Kundry as seductress; this violin solo has that quality of arabesque, seen also in Ex. 7, which lends so much to the quintessential quality of *Jeux*.

Ex. 10c i   *Jeux*, f.s., pp. 28-9

Ex. 10c ii   *Jeux*, f.s., p. 36

Ex. 10c iii   *Jeux*, f.s., p. 45
(cf. also Ex. 6b ii)

Ex. 10d   *Jeux*, f.s., pp. 74-5

Ex. 10e   *Parsifal*, m.s., pp. 580-81

The next example is concerned with Debussy's more complex use of the same idea. Ex. 11a is the Dresden Amen from *Parsifal*, quoted here in E♭. 11b shows it in one of its least simple guises, as it comes, extended so as to rise two octaves, rhythmically distorted, harmonically severely disturbed from its native E♭, in the prelude to Act III. The effect of this passage is overwhelming as the Dresden Amen reaches a discord instead of its culminating concord, and topples down Kundry's descending motif over nearly three octaves, into a powerful transformation of Parsifal's 'pure fool' motif. A few pages later we are forcibly reminded that this descent does indeed belong to Kundry, as Gurnemanz revives

Ex. 11a   *Parsifal* (The Dresden Amen)

Ex. 11b   *Parsifal*, m.s., pp. 669-70

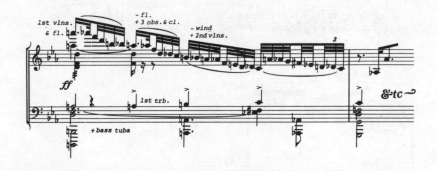

her and she utters a cry. This passage, Ex. 11c, also consists of a version of the Dresden Amen in E♭ (the harmonization is now very close to the original Ex. 11a), again interrupted at the top by a dissonant chord, this time ' Kundry's chord ', and downward rush. Here the rush comes to an end on a long-held horn note, followed by the passage quoted as Ex. 5a of Chapter V, the pattering figure of Kundry hesitant and timorous. A few bars later comes the tail-end of the present quotation, the little figure on two clarinets in thirds which later accompanies her muttered 'dienen, dienen'. The first four bars of Ex. 11d are the climax of the jeune homme's attentions to the second girl in *Jeux*. In the passage that follows, of which the first seven bars are quoted, they notice

Ex. 11c   *Parsifal*, m.s., pp 682-4

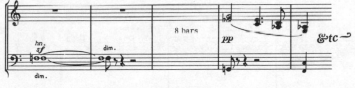

the anxiety and pique of the abandoned first girl, and the second
tries to win her back. The first four bars are in fact four such
attempts to reach the top of the Dresden Amen as seen in both
these extracts from the opening of *Parsifal* Act III. The key also—
E♭ —is the same. Then the rush down, marked 'expressif et
éperdu', 'distracted', beginning with a Kundry-like violence on
all the first violins, and rapidly reducing in speed, volume and
number of players until by bar 9 only a solo violin[1] is left with
any indication of motion; not pattering, as with Kundry's figure,
but 'inquiète, puis chagriné'[2] perhaps, and certainly timid and
hesitant. Then follows the little figure on two clarinets in thirds

1. The full score omits this instruction.
2. See scenario.

Ex. 11d *Jeux*, f.s., pp. 71-3

which presumably is the start of the second girl's entreaties, at
first resisted but in the end successful, to take the first girl in her
arms. Gurnemanz also carries the frozen Kundry out of the
bushes, rubs her hands and temples, and awakes her to life;[1]

1. *Parsifal*, v.s. pp. 218-9.

moreover the girl in *Jeux* is restored to 'service', for the jeune homme joins the two girls, 'en écartant leurs têtes doucement', and as the scenario delicately puts it, they 'abandon themselves to their fantasy'—the triple dance and the triple kiss.

If this connection seems forced—if anyway it seems unbecoming, on the 'holiest day of all' and in the 'pleasant open spring landscape in the domains of the Grail', to resurrect the devastated magic garden of devilish women—I have to insist that these parallels follow the direction patently taken by the music. When the re-creation of an original passage in *Parsifal* is so direct and vivid as this, it is in order to clarify the nature of the *musical* connection that all the less obvious verbal and associative connections are made; to clarify, and also, if possible, to give a meaning. If however a more fitting source is needed for the kiss which binds the three nymphs together at the climax of *Jeux*, 'confounding them in an ecstasy' very different from that experienced during Kundry's kissing of Parsifal (or vice versa),[1] it is easily to be found in *Tristan*. Ex. 12a gives the familiar phrase, at the same pitch as it occurs in the climactic bars of *Jeux*—Ex. 12b. The same phrase returns thereafter three times (12c) as if obsessed with these three notes but now, after the climax subsides and the memory fades (see Ex. 6c), unable to launch them on the rising sequential journey they initiate in the Wagner.

Ex. 12a   *Tristan*

Ex. 12b   *Jeux*, f.s., p. 113

1. *Parsifal*, v.s. p. 184; p. 253.

Ex. 12c   *Jeux*, f.s., pp. 113-14

(In the piano score this passage is marked 'avec une expression doucement appuyée'.)

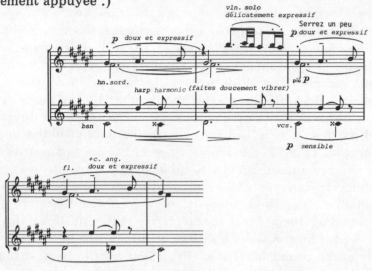

Now Exx. 10 and 11 are all concerned with the presence in *Jeux* of one theme from *Parsifal*—Kundry's downward rush, shown in its basic form in Ex. 10a. This motif is usually employed to suggest fury and despair; but Ex. 10b showed that it could also be used to suggest enticement and languishment, thus bringing it close to some of the most frequent effects in *Jeux*. Ex. 10e, also a Kundry-languishing passage, possesses 'that quality of arabesque which lends so much to the quintessential quality of *Jeux*.' In fact Exx. 10b and e form a continuous passage, the music of which repeats and extends the setting of the dialogue between Kundry and Klingsor about her subservience and his chastity, quoted above. But the words of *this* passage (v.s. pp. 190-2) are sung by a horrified Parsifal as Kundry 'bends over him with the caressing movements that are here denoted'; and these words[1] (and movements) run:

> Aye! With this accent, so called she him; and this her look, truly I know it well, this also, to him unpeaceful smiling; so tempted, aye, was he by her lips, so too her neck was bending;

---

1. Always in Margaret Glyn's quaint but felicitous translation.

so boldly rose her head; so lightly her locks fluttered o'er him, so wound she her arm round his neck; so flattering smiled her features; in league with every pang of anguish, his soul's salvation her mouth did kiss away!

These words of Parsifal have not been withheld to make a belated connection between the actions of the jeune homme and the girls round about figs. 49-51 in *Jeux*, and Gurnemanz's restoration of warmth to the frozen Kundry. Rather they serve as a reminder of the urgency of the seductive element in *Parsifal* which the banter of *Jeux*'s treatment of the same thing is likely to dissipate. Kundry (to adopt the terminology of Wieland Wagner's 'Psychological Diagram for *Parsifal*') is a 'seductress against her will', 'under the hallucination that release will come through physical abandonment to him whom she believes to be the saviour'; she has laughed at God on the Cross, she has profaned the Cup, she is engaged in a tireless search for grace and absolution. She is in bondage to Klingsor, whose 'absence of faith', 'chaos of egotism' and 'desperate struggle against sensuality' have caused him to mutilate himself, without in any way bettering his condition. The true instrument of his quietus in destruction and Kundry's in salvation is Parsifal, who at the moment of his contact with Klingsor and Kundry is at the crucial point of his spiritual development; the combination of guilt towards his mother and the misery of sensuality he learns from Kundry's kiss lead to a recognition of his greater guilt towards the Erlöser, which must now be expiated in a life of suffering and sacrifice.

It is to these aspects of the opera that the examples I have discussed from *Jeux* are related. The sphere of Amfortas and Titurel is not present, but the central progress in the work of which they are a part—Parsifal's advance over the ramparts, through the garden of girls, through Kundry, then Klingsor, to complete selfawareness and acceptance of his fulfilment-in-renunciation—is what *Jeux* refers to and what it expresses.

In Chapter II I said that '*Parsifal* is the instrument of Debussy's achievement of his profoundest aims'; and in the chapter on *Le Martyre*, that Debussy produces in *Jeux* 'a coherent, if still selective, amalgam of the richness of psychological meaning and musical material in all three acts of *Parsifal*.' *Jeux* is indeed a re-creation of Wagner's allegory brought about by an assimilation of his music so thorough (within the limits of its predilection) that paradoxically, it has all but disappeared. It leaves behind not the cluttered débris of an influence, but a diaphony radically original though everywhere suffused with what has passed through. The relation from *Parsifal* to *Jeux* consists in the musical connections I have just set forth; but to see the *meaning* of *Jeux* the process must be reversed, taking the elements of *Jeux* back to their sources in *Parsifal*, where not to interpret is to avoid the music's intent.

Debussy's 'artistic "manners" '[1] find the vastness, wholeness, and deliberate profundity of this kind of art to be antipathetic. That his 'manners' involve diminution of the original is obviously true; but this is scarcely the point. Debussy's extraordinary achievement is to hold the sexual thralldom and the yearning for redemption, everything agonizing in Wagner's subject, in a lucid suspension. This subject-matter is there, but not openly so; it is not even presented, let alone explored—this for the mature Debussy would be simply 'bad manners'—rather it is there, by subtle association, by delicate assimilation, as an unconscious presence of which the elucidation is perhaps bound to be crass.

Jeux takes *Parsifal* and leavens it with such diaphanous *pudeur* that, as Debussy remarked, 'any hint of immorality escapes through the feet of the *danseuse* and ends in a pirouette'.'

4. Subject-Matter and Meaning

It is now possible again to consider the question first raised by the scenario of *Jeux*—the question of how the work can be profound when the pretext for it, its ostensible plot, is so very slender. Quotations from various sources will help me towards an answer.

First a few more phrases (italics always mine) from Eimert's article on *Jeux* to which I have already referred. Eimert's analysis is more subtle than the conclusions he draws from it; his remarks set up that kind of psychological reverberation which defines a new apprehension of a work's significance. '*Lack of meaning in*

---

1. Vladimir Nabokov: (compare Stravinsky; ' my manners are my personal relations with my material. ')

thematic terms becomes true significance . . .'; again, ' . . . In their *tender evocativeness and psychological delicacy* such arabesques, modelled on the stage-action, touch on *something almost inexplicable*; the more so since their strikingly concrete effect can *hardly be explained by any deep-seated interpretation* . . .'; and again, ' . . . the sound of *Jeux* . . . which for all its extreme refinement . . . remains linked in a natural way to the world . . . *without detours via functions of meaning, without a false emphasis on "depth".* '

Secondly, a quotation from an early letter of Wittgenstein, with comments upon it by its recipient, Paul Engelmann:

> The poem by Uhland[1] is really magnificent. And this is how it is; if only you do not try to utter what is unutterable then *nothing* gets lost. But the unutterable will be—unutterably—contained in what has been uttered.

Upon this Engelmann comments:

> The 'positive' achievement of Wittgenstein, is his pointing to what is manifest in a proposition. And what is manifest in it, a proposition cannot also state explicitly. The poet's sentences, for instance, achieve their effect not through what they say but through what is manifest in them, and the same holds for music, which also says nothing.

My purpose in this section is to attempt penetrating the diaphony of *Jeux* to interpret the hidden Wagnerian sources which the previous section brought to light. Eimert—with his insistence on the non-content of *Jeux* ('lack of meaning . . . becomes true significance', etc.)—keeps in mind the danger of a too unremittingly technical or aesthetic view of a work of art. Engelmann and Wittgenstein keep a more 'positive' side in view, that the vitality of the utterance consists in its holding deep in its recesses the implicit 'unutterable', Located somewhere between the two is Freud's 'interaction of latent and manifest content'. *Jeux* is a work in which plot is reduced almost to a nothing, and subject-matter remains entirely latent. But its 'manifest content'—the rhythmic delicacy and harmonic refinement, the suavely suggestive contour of its melodic arabesques, the consummate radiance and liveliness of its orchestra; in a word, the music—is not 'all that is the case'. With delight we hear and understand the 'manifest content', yet in it—actually diffused in it rather than concealed somehow be-

---

1. *Graf Eberhards Weissdorn.*

neath, or beyond, or behind—is the profundity of meaning, the implicit utterance that cannot be uttered.

To return now to the notion left unresolved at the end of the first section of this chapter, that *Jeux* is without subject, or at best, that its subject is itself, is to see that it is extraordinarily mistaken. *Jeux*, for several decades after its première neglected, indeed written-off as an indication of its composer's declining powers, is now widely regarded as absolutely central both to Debussy's oeuvre and to subsequent developments in composition. But all considerations of the work concentrate solely on the music. Necessarily so, of course; for the qualities in *Jeux* that have made it of such seminal importance to the music of the 1950s and '60s *avant-garde* are hardly to be studied in the scenario. Nevertheless an essential dimension is missing if the scenario and the music are not considered as illuminating each other. If they are separated for purposes of analysis, it is vital that the attempt be made to bring them together again. Otherwise the work falls to bits; the music *per se* is either 'tremors and swoons . . . cries of anguished voluptuousness' (David Drew) or else an important milestone on the road to *Le marteau sans maître* and *Pli selon pli*, according to whether the work is viewed in its period or with hindsight. And the scenario *per se* is of course a mere nothing, a 'sexy' mood-piece at most (Wilfrid Mellers).

They must be taken together; and when they are the result, while more than the 'manifest content', is still not the totality of the work's meaning. For it could still, even at this stage, be objected that the scenario is 'idiotic'. The music and the scenario, inseparable as they are, are given their totality of meaning only when the presence of the subject-matter of *Parsifal* is understood. The subject-matter of *Parsifal* (present in all the ways I have analysed in the previous section) is the 'unutterable—unutterably contained in what has been uttered'; it is the latent content whose presence gives the manifest everything that can be discovered there of meaning and profundity, as in stained glass the picture is contained within the glass and cannot be extracted and considered separately from it yet the effect is hardly at all of a representation of a specific subject but one of light and colour alone.

And what then *is* this meaning, towards whose 'unutterable' 'right word' I have striven so long? The music of *Jeux* is inseparable from its subject-matter, which is sexual pleasure.

CHAPTER IX

CONJUNCTION

Introduction

For you who understand there can . . . be nothing in what follows there ought not to be. My story, if I have one (and in that very speculation there seems to be so much of it), must, after all, be clarity itself to those from whom it is written, who are so exactly not those who would hesitate or boggle at a meaning . . . It was deep; deeper, you know, a good deal than I was, or even am; so that, in the end, I found and perhaps still find myself swimming upon an ocean whose profundity it is altogether impossible to gauge. What he found — or whether he found anything at all — are questions which, though they add immensely to the complication — might perhaps eventually lead to a solution of the whole thing. At any rate it is certain that whatever interest my story has centres round just two persons, two characters, two phases. Its fascination is that it holds a perpetual antithesis between two such wonderful contraries . . .[1]

I want in this final chapter to attempt an interpretation of the relationship between Debussy and Wagner. To do this, it will be necessary to get beyond both the biographical relation sketched in section 4 of Chapter I, and the analytic connections dealt with in the chapters that follow. I am no longer concerned with the historic Wagner (1813-83) nor the historic Debussy (1862-1918) so much as the area (an area of subject-matter and style, needless to add, rather than, for instance, the years 1862-83) where they converge. My interpretation arises out of the material in earlier chapters; but once this material is established, it suggests insights which cannot be covered by analysis alone.

1. From an early parody of James by Lytton Strachey (quoted in Holroyd's life of Strachey, Vol. I, pp. 133-4).

Conjunction

1. *Debussy's 'Wagnerian Works'*

My analyses have dealt with a portion only of the works of
Debussy, and have related them to only one aspect, though a
central one, of Wagner's wide range. This perhaps does not require
explanation; it would be pointless to attempt to find the
impression of Wagner in those aspects of Debussy — essential, and
for many quintessential, to his oeuvre — which derive from
Mussorgsky and Borodin, the Balinese gamelan, or Spain; which are
set in play by Japanese prints and Chinoiserie, or the paintings of
Turner, Whistler, and the Impressionists; or which return in fancy
to the spirit of the French seventeenth and eighteenth centuries.
These are facets of Debussy's work which are well-received and
acknowledged; they are developed in conscious antithesis to and
reaction from anything Wagnerian.

His works here analyzed, however, though chosen initially
because they appeared to contain references both musical and of
subject-matter to Wagner which could be isolated and described,
have by now a certain identity of their own. They make a genre,
among all the other genres in Debussy's oeuvre: they could be
called 'Debussy's Wagnerian Works'. Of course such an invented
category can by no means be hard and fast. What makes a work by
Debussy one of his 'Wagnerian Works' is a certain ambience of
subject-matter and musical style which however Debussyan it
seems both at first and in the end, can nonetheless be traced to a
Wagnerian source and be shown to be in some kind of pregnant
relationship to the subject-matter and musical style of the appropriate Wagnerian original. That they are absolutely at the centre
of his 'output is surely clear — neither the oriental nor the Spanish
nor the broadly 'impressionist' works can rival a category which
boasts major aspects of *La Damoiselle élue*, the *Cinq Poèmes*,
Pelléas, and *Jeux*.

Apart from brief incursions into the *Ring* noted in their place,
Debussy's relation to Wagner is confined to *Tristan* and *Parsifal*.
Even here, not to the totality of subject-matter and musical
content of these works; Debussy's view of them, though intense, is
decidedly partial. That he found in the original only the specialities
for which he had a predilection led him to reject alien aspects of
Wagner, the epic grandeur of the *Ring* equally with the warm
Brahmsian-Straussian vein of *Die Meistersinger*. *Lohengrin*, and

196

especially *Tannhäuser,* do treat the subject-matter Debussy and Wagner hold in common; but here the musical style (as well as the genre of Romantic Opera) is well outside Debussy's range of interest. 'Rejection' would be the wrong word for his attitude to the aspects of Wagner which achieve full expression outside *Tristan* and *Parsifal.* Were it not for the fact that temporal proximity, and the contemporary French view of Wagner, placed him in the relation described in Chapter I, Debussy would probably have regarded the 'German' side (so to speak) of Wagner with frigid tranquillity.

For it must be noted, though without attaching undue weight to the fact, that whereas all Wagner's other works derive from Nordic or Teutonic mythology (in *Die Meisteringer,* German history), the stories of *Tristan* and *Parsifal* are Franco-Celtic in origin, though not in their most elaborate medieval treatment. The idea of a 'French' as opposed to a Nordic-Teutonic Wagner gives a further implication to Nietzsche's mordant declaration[1] '. . . it is . . . glaringly obvious, that Paris is the very *soil* for him'. It is not so much that there might still, after so many centuries, be some kind of instinctive recognition that these romances are native whereas the other myths are so blatantly *boches;* rather, that the plots of *Tristan* and *Parsifal,* taken with the psychological depths that Wagner's treatment allows them to sustain, will be bound to appeal to 'l'âme moderne'. This is what 'l'âme moderne' has added to the evolution of sensibility. Even Nietzsche's perversity could not go so far as to attribute 'all that thrills . . . extravagant caresses . . . all the femininity from the vocabulary of happiness',[2] to *Die Meistersinger* or the *Ring!* Whereas on any view they have a vital place in both *Tristan* and *Parsifal,* and in the French view, they are of the essence.

What, now, is the 'ambience of subject-matter and musical style' which Debussy's Wagnerian works share with each other, and with the aspects of *Tristan* and *Parsifal* from which they so significantly depend? The answer, put as briefly as possible, is the making explicit in music of the inward and outward motions of sexuality. This is what

1. See p. 1.
2. See p.1.

Debussy and Wagner, in as much as they overlap with each other, are concerned with, and this, in as much as the statement can be made about music, is what their music is 'powerful to express'.[1] I have already committed myself to expressions of this in Debussy's case; does the same thing have to be spelled out in the case of Wagner? From the earliest it has been recognized, whether the word has been uttered or not,[2] that 'unquenchable sensuality' is central to the subject of *Tristan;* and that *Parsifal* is a drama of renunciation in which, after a representation perhaps the most gorgeous and psychologically far-penetrating ever made of what is supposed to be relinquished, even the expression of religious longing, life-long quest, and final attainment, are permeated with the ardour of the carnality they ostensibly deny.

It comes down to a duality, a conflict between the Chaste and the Erotic. The latter has never been better put than by Baudelaire:—

> . . . languors, fevered and agonized delights, ceaseless returns towards an ecstasy of pleasure which promises to quench but never does quench, thirst; frenzied palpitations of heart and senses, imperious orders of the flesh, the whole onomatopoeic dictionary of Love is to be heard here.

This[3] was of course written about *Tannhäuser,* where the conflict is set out with black and white crudity. Though the conflict is an important element in Act III, *Tristan* fundamentally devotes itself to what Baudelaire describes; only in *Parsifal* is it covered fully and explicitly, not in black and white, but in a scheme that ranges from deepest purples to dove-grey and swan-white.

Once the case of Wagner is delineated so specifically, we can imagine how Debussy's instinctive artistic manners will transform it. Another quotation[4] indicates the *simple* reaction:—

> I listened to *Pelléas et Mélisande.* I know nothing about music; but I compared the words of the old libretti ('I pay with my blood for the love I reposed in you'), gross, blood-battered, heavy words — with the words of Pelléas and Mélisande ('j'ai froid — ta chevelure') — fleeting, aquatic words. *From tiredness*

---

1. 'Music is, by its very nature, essentially powerless to express anything at all'. Further exception to this famous view will be taken below.

2. See p. 64.

3. 'Richard Wagner and Tannhäuser in Paris'.

4. Natalia Ginzberg: *Silenzio* (translated Jehane Burns; my italics).

and disgust with large bloody words have come these watery,
cold, evasive words.

The purpose of this concluding chapter is to define the more
complex reaction that establishes a Conjunction between Debussy
and Wagner.

2. *A Conjunction of Different Artistic 'Manners'*

Debussy and Wagner manifest in complementary fashion the
opposite ways of understanding and holding an attitude towards
the subject-matter they have in common. Discussion of this stems
from the passing reference to artistic manners at the end of the
third section of the Chapter on *Jeux:*-'Debussy's artistic "manners" '
find antipathetic the vastness, wholeness, and overt profundity 'of
Wagner's kind of art'; and further '. . . this subject-matter (of
Parsifal) is there, but not openly so; it is not even "presented", let
alone "explored" — this for the mature Debussy would be simply
"bad manners" '.[1] Important aspects of the Wagner-Debussy Conjunction can be elicited by extending this notion of artistic
manners (using the word now in its conventional as well as its
metaphorical meaning) to make *civilization* into an ideal as
valuable and desirable in artistic as it is in social terms.

Civilization in this sense represents a repression of the vigorous
and direct — not so much in the actual choice of subject-matter, as
in its capacity to bear 'ideas', to be 'meaningful'; and also in the
way it wishes to present itself, and is able to present itself at all,
in the work of art. It is as if there were a lower and an upper
storey of rooms. In the lower room the manner is argumentative,
'committed', full of content and significance, expressed with
'masculine persuasive force'. Above in the upper room good taste
reigns (the 'feminine of genius'); the same subject might be
broached, but in a refined manner, with nothing charmlessly
didactic or tediously heavy in tone or in content. However high
and elegant the upper room, and however turgid and boorish the
lower, there is still a connection of the greatest directness between
them; without the lower, the upper would fall. The high-civilized

1. See p. 192.

manner is a precious bloom (precious often enough in both senses) which emanates from the earthiness of the low-civilized manner, however much it rarifies it, and whatever the eventual distance between them. Moreover it is strictly a one-way commerce; 'by some inexplicable phenomenon, light needs darkness, but darkness has no need of light'.

The upper-room manner is thin, elegant, refined, delicate, subtly disclaiming: the lower-room, energetic, powerful, expansive, consciously searching and profound. To the low, the condition of high-civilization will seem vapid, lacking in both passion and understanding — and if the worst comes to the worst, fundamentally inessential. To the high, the low-civilized condition will seem crude, ugly, over-loaded, lacking suavity and decent restraint. But on the other hand the high cannot call the low inessential; it must always hold itself, whether willingly or not, in some kind of relation to, or reaction from, the lower state which in gravity it rests upon. Even if it flouts its origins it merely thereby acknowledges their power; the worst it can do is affect to ignore or despise.

Applying this set of complements to a couple of contemporaries like D. H. Lawrence the coal-miner's son and Ronald Firbank the coal-miner's grandson, results in an antithesis unexceptionable indeed, but hardly illuminating. It would be a closed circuit, not carrying possibilities of understanding the antithesis any further. A simple *contrast* of manners says that Lawrence rants and swears in the lower room while Firbank titters and suspires in the upper. The contrast is only significant when there is a *relation* between the two floors. With Debussy and Wagner the lower and upper room image is an emblem of what it means to link them together at all. In their Conjunction, they are both talking about the same subject, according to these very different but complementary modes of behaviour.

A central formulation of the upper-room manner is Eliot's description of James. He speaks of James's 'baffling escape from Ideas', which he finds 'perhaps the last test of a superior intelligence. He had a mind so fine that no idea could violate it'.[1] Some formulation like this has obviously stood behind my attempt in

1. T. S. Eliot: *In Memory of Henry James* (reprinted in Edmund Wilson's *The Shock of Recognition*).

Chapter VIII to show that *Jeux* was a sort of latent suspension of the richness and explicitness (rather than the Ideas as such) of *Parsifal*. Now here again, the more interesting possibility, in the case of Wagner and Debussy, is not the contrast between the man who has ideas and the man who transcends them; but rather, the relation between their different attitude towards and achievement of a similar subject. And if the interest focuses upon the relation rather than the antithesis, the general value of Eliot's formulation of intelligence (attractive as it is) becomes somewhat tendentious. To succumb to its attractions would be to say that Debussy's relative emptiness of content is not an expression of his manners, but of his 'superior intelligence', to the absence of which can be attributed Wagner's concern with fullness of content in a manner which must consequently be called coarse. The obvious rejoinder would be, that Wagner's greatness, and superior intelligence, are shown not least in his baffling *mastery* of ideas. (I refer not to the amateur and pundit of world-philosophy, but the artist who knew just what to set, and what to omit, in Brünnhilde's final speech in *Götterdämmerung*).

Two further misapprehensions must be avoided in this context. The first, suggested by a movement away from Eliot's remark, is to find only the lower room capable of intellectual seriousness, and the upper only of frivolity. Here, while the lower certainly bears the weight, the upper is also serious, according to an entirely different view of the possibilities of being so. This leads to the second misapprehension, the question of taste. Of course, in my emblem of the two complementary modes of civilization, Debussy would be the embodiment of good taste, while Wagner would burst brutally through its constrictions. This duality of good taste, frivolity and light seriousness, versus earnestness and tastelessness could be taken further and be presented in terms of the stereotyped German picture of the French (tastefulness, a talent to amuse, champagne, naughtiness, can-cans, *Carmen*[1]) and the stereotyped French picture of the German (turgid profundity, stupidity, grossness, tastelessness, bombast, counterpoint, sausage-

1. Compare de Ternant's spoof which has Debussy, aet. 25, meet Brahms, who drinks champagne, quotes *Faust* on the subject:
   Ein echter deutscher Mann mag keinen Franzen leiden
   Doch ihre Weine trinkt er gern
   and takes the young man to see *Carmen,* claiming he would go to the end of the earth to embrace Bizet! (Lockspeiser, *Master Musicians* volume pp. 44-5).

eating). But these kinds of antithesis are culs-de-sac too. Consideration of whether one is tasteful and the other not will not shed any
further light on the relation of Debussy and Wagner. And anyway,
what is taste? To say that Debussy and Wagner share a taste for
the subject-matter they have in common; that Wagner's taste will
be for one kind of manner in treating it, and Debussy's for another,
antithetical but complementary manner; and that to Debussy
Wagner's manners would be tasteless (that is, distasteful in their
boldness and expansion) and that to Wagner Debussy's manners
would be tasteless (that is, insipid, empty both of *Schwung* and
substance) — this would be moving towards significant antitheses
and complements. What I have in mind is the Conjunction which
embodies both modes of civilization and makes them the identical
thing, deflected into opposite directions by differences of tone,
attitude, and purpose.

Of course as soon as it is called 'the identical thing' it must, if it
is to make sense at all, be subject to the most strenuous definitions
and distinctions. And of course, in the end, the differences between
Wagner and Debussy are so great as to force me to confess what
is anyway obvious from the start — that however nearly Debussy
approaches Wagner in subject-matter and musical material, there is
not for a moment, even when he uses Wagner virtually verbatim,
any question of his being 'the identical thing'. Substantial as his
debt clearly is, his different manners make what he has taken into
something absolutely other. If then it is the differences which
distinguish and delineate, why expend such energy in a foredoomed effort to make the two composers appear the same? The
answer is, that only by a temporary insistence upon the similarity
can the differences be elicited in their most complex and illuminating form. To insist upon the difference from the start both
states the obvious, and checks any possible further discovery.

So for a moment it is possible to suspend received truths, and to
regard 'the facts' as incidental. Debussy and Wagner form a
conjunction quite distinct from (though overlapping with) the
historic case of the influence of the older master upon his junior,
documented earlier. A conjunction of this other kind could be
effected across the centuries, and across cultures differing much
more fundamentally than the French and the German. It consists
of a relationship formed of a complex of connections, some

similarities, some antitheses, some comparisons and contrasts, here incompatible there complementary. In it each member can be defined in terms of the other, and descriptions can be found which link them together in significant ways; these definitions and descriptions will be to the benefit of them both, that is, will enable them both to be grasped in a more complete and far-reaching way. This extra-historical conjunction between Wagner and Debussy, when combined with the factual one with which I have so far been largely concerned, produces their Conjunction; this Conjunction is great with meanings which can only be apprehended by causing it to exist at all.

Their common subject-matter, the Erotic, and the struggle between the Erotic and the Chaste, is seen by Wagner with the manners that render it rich, full, and explicit; the conscious embodiment of ideas and emotions aiming to express, and give significance to, the human condition. Debussy's treatment of just the same subject has undergone a metamorphosis into the manners of the upper room; light, teasing, unacknowledging, empty of ideas, restrained in feelings, and shy of overt expression.

3. *Effect upon Audience*

An important aspect of the Debussy – Wagner Conjunction, their different manners towards their audience, arises out of the preceding section. Debussy's two principal Wagnerian works will serve as examples. In *Pelléas* Debussy sets the 'plot' to music, and it is up to the audience, individual by individual, to elicit the 'subject-matter', and beyond it the 'meaning', which inhere within the plot. In *Jeux* the subject-matter and meaning (and plot also, remembering its scenario!) have become subtly dissolved into the diaphonous glow and evanescence of the music itself. For Debussy to have depicted directly the *Parsifal*-emotions present in *Jeux* by implication might well have been to steer dangerously near to undisclosed elements (undisclosed whether deliberately or unconsciously) of his personality. In other words, 'bad manners'. *Jeux* escapes once more with a pirouette.

The surface of *Pelléas* is deliberately flat, and its depths unplumbed, in order that the emotion, rather than emanating from the work outwards towards its corporate audience, might be centred instead in individual after individual who, in hearing it, brings to it from his own resources the sensitivity of response it requires. The work itself is incomplete; it has to be filled out by those listeners who vibrate to it with sympathetic understanding; only then does it acquire full substantiality. Four diverse illustrations help to amplify this point; an axiom of Jean-Luc Godard that 'what is alive is not what's on the screen, but *what is between the audience and the screen*'. Another film-maker – Mamoulian's request to Garbo to make her face for the final sequence of *Queen Christina* 'like a blank piece of paper. I want the writing to be done by every member of the audience'. Third, Clarisse in *The Man Without Qualities* – 'take music, for instance . . . we draw the experiences towards ourselves and spread them out again in the same movement. *We want ourselves . . .* '; and finally, Mauriac – 'music . . . compels us to see nothing but what it has discovered in ourselves, which is always the most secret, the most deeply buried part of us . . .'

Therefore Henry James's definition of works whose content is *thin* ('thin – because everywhere asking more of the imagination than they can be detected in giving it'[1]) cannot be advanced as a charge against Debussy's insubstantiality. His thinness has a special function and value; it extends the possibility of the manner in which an artist is able to employ the imaginations of those individuals who comprise his audience, and make them collaborators in the affectingness of his effects. The ideal *Pelléas*tre will do his own writing upon the blank features of the music, and, in bringing himself to it in passive collaboration, will discover revealed in himself just those secret motions that he desires to discover and has the capacity to. He will need to bring more than the artist usually expects his audience to bring, that is, a power of imaginative projection, an ability to suspend disbelief. He must contain, however deep-buried, the very qualities in his inner emotional life which the work perhaps involuntarily lays bare and plays upon. When this is done, the work is no longer insubstantial. Its fullness of effect is a kind of bargain between its creator, and his listeners' capacity for recognizing in themselves certain virtually inarticulate feelings. Debussy's art 'n'impose rien, ne propose rien' – he

1. *The American Scene*, original edition p. 442.

exposes the emotions with which he deals, but exposes them in his listeners rather than presenting them fully embodied in his own work of art. Perhaps this is what Auden means when he says that *Pelléas* 'succeeds only because it flatters the audience'. This superficially silly remark is in fact profoundly true. Without the right listeners to appeal to, *Pelléas* wilts and dies.

In Wagner, on the contrary, the work is sufficient unto itself, a complete embodiment of every aspect of what it sets out to express. For Wagner, who with his bold understanding of the function and workings of myth wrote his own texts because nobody else could have envisaged what he needed, the Plot expresses its subject-matter, the Subject-matter is the plot exteriorized, while the music so wholeheartedly devotes itself to the intensification of their utterance that in it the events of which the Plot and the emotions of which the Subject consist find their fullest and most expressive embodiment. Meaning in Wagner *(pace* the prodigious wealth of 'unconscious' interpretations that can be adduced) is primarily direct and fully self-cognizant. This manner of presentation is at its most complete in *Tristan* and *Parsifal;* here more than in the epic grandeurs of the *Ring* the music 'represents the emotional disturbance itself and demands that for its fullest comprehension its hearers shall infer the cause'.[1]

Wagner's hearers are plainly an audience, a collective noun rather than the individuals who comprise it. This could be guessed from the style and presentation of his work alone, even if it were not an attested artistic ideal that he wished, like the ancient Athenian drama, to involve the Folk as a whole. For Wagner's works to achieve their effect his audience has to sacrifice its passivity and its possibilities of scrupulous withdrawal into private reserves of emotion. It must yield up both collaboration and resistance, and succumb to the superabundant sway of Wagner's manner, in which everything is present, fully explicit and fully worked, and expressed to its uttermost intensity. He indeed both proposes and imposes; the emotion that the work evokes is already embodied in the work itself; the music is the effect it makes, it is its own meaning, in its presentation of itself and all it contains. Far from flattering his audience, Wagner belabours them by leaving nothing

---

1. D. Ferguson, quoted in Suzanne Langer, *Philosophy in a New Key.*

to the imagination — they must yield to the victorious amplitude of an art where the word is made flesh.[1] Any listener who seeks to preserve independence of judgement, of consciousness even, would be better off in the upper room.

Wagner's and Debussy's complementary relations to their audience can be summarized like this: that in the case of Wagner, it is in what he brings to his audience that the significance lies, in Debussy's, it is in what his audience brings to him. The haunting line in Coleridge's *Dejection-Ode* —

O Lady, we receive but what we give

puts the Debussyan attitude in a nutshell. In Wagner we receive what he gives us.

4. *Debussy's Wagnerian Works Reconsidered*

While their tendency was always towards the interpretative hint or generalizing statement, it was nonetheless outside the immediate scope of the earlier chapters to attempt more than an analysis of the musical and verbal connections between Wagner and Debussy. Here I take up those hints and develop those statements, relegating the analytical work to the background. As a background the analyses are of course a *sine qua non*, and I take it as assumed that whatever I shall go on to develop derives from material that has already been fully presented.

Behind the earliest works of Debussy is an ideal of pleasure. Even in the little songs and piano pieces written before his style was able to incorporate the parallel ninths with which he used to shock his contemporaries and elders at the Conservatoire by calling 'mon plaisir',[2] the characteristic mood is already established. His ability gradually to employ the ninths and higher discords was commensurate with his expression of pleasure becoming more various, complex, and interesting; in effect, more *pleasurable* — new modes of taking pleasure, new objects in which pleasure may

1. The words of the *Liebestod*:-
   In dem wogenden Schwall, in dem tönenden Schall,
   In des Welt Atems wehendem All—
   ertrinken, versinken......
   best evoke Wagner's characteristic effect on the audience.

2. See pp. 30 - 31.

be felt. The earliest works where Debussy finds his musical individuality are also those where pleasure is celebrated as the 'first and sovereign good'; their motto might be the opening of the Verlaine setting which first spreads out a lingering ninth, eleventh, thirteenth, for our unashamed delight[1] –

> C'est l'extase langoureuse –

and we might add to this his declaration that 'Music should humbly seek to please . . . beauty must appeal to the senses, must provide us with immediate enjoyment, must impress us or insinuate itself into us without any effort on our part'.

The next line of the Verlaine (only at the end of which does the harmony find any kind of linguistically-sanctioned resting-place) –

> C'est la fatigue amoureuse

–focuses more precisely an important aspect of the Debussyan idea of pleasure; the ecstasy is languid, the amour is weary. How much this is simply a commonplace in the verse of Verlaine and of the period as a whole, and how much Debussy's sensibility at this early stage is inseparable from that of the poets he set, are not really the questions here. The point is, rather, to note Debussy's attraction again and again to images of sleepy voluptuousness, revealing an idea of sensual pleasure which tends downwards towards unconsciousness out of sheer languor, rather than reaching up towards it in idealistic aspiration. There is much to encourage such a tendency in *Tristan* and *Parsifal*.

Up to his early maturity Debussy's penchant for pleasure, and for Wagner, is more or less within the conventional expectations of his times and place. But he develops into a composer so idiosyncratic – one critic has gone so far as to call him a 'mutation' – that both the commonplace idea of pleasure which forms part of his artistic background, and the conventional French view of Wagner in which he grew up, are transformed into something new. This newness, however, although inexplicable *merely* in terms of the commonplaces which at first fostered it and in which it first expressed itself, can always be related back to its origins however far it voyages from them.

1. See Ch. VIII Ex. 1d.

The *Cinq Poèmes de Charles Baudelaire* and *La Damoiselle élue* are the first works where Debussy, in pursuing his predilection both for Wagner and for pleasure, diverges from what could have been predicted from the conventionalities of his time and place. The *Cinq Poèmes* is the work in which he most nearly approaches — approaches as nearly as he *can* — both the matter and the manner of those aspects of Wagner which he finds appealing. Clearly this congruity is comparable to Baudelaire's own sympathy, a generation earlier, with just the same aspects of Wagner. The man who could write in such terms[1] about the original *Tannhäuser* overture (not even the new Paris Bacchanale) had no need of *Tristan* to reveal to him his *ardeurs*. In the *Cinq Poèmes* Debussy and Baudelaire under the tutelage of 'le dieu Richard Wagner' join forces to produce a work of which Nietzsche's Wagner-descriptions — the 'wealth of colour, of chiaroscuro, of the mystery of a dying light' which 'so pampers our senses that afterwards almost every other musician strikes us as being too robust'[2] — really do, at last, seem to be true.

Not only do Nietzsche's words beautifully convey the erotic ambience of the Debussy Baudelaire settings, but, as so often, they carry quite the wrong suggestion about Wagner. Wagner is as robust, both in *minutiae* and in overall span, as a Victorian railway station — it is after him that a composer like Debussy strikes us as being almost too shrinking and reserved! The characteristic French tendency, shown at one of its great moments in Debussy's collaboration with Baudelaire, is away both from the polemic of the chastity versus sensuality struggle as portrayed in *Tannhäuser*, and from the 'philosophy' of night-worship and love-death embraced in *Tristan*, towards the 'pampering' of the *extase langoureuse* and the 'dying' of the *fatigue amoureuse*. For Debussy the beginning of the *Tristan* love-duet[3] is how things should remain, poised in timeless *volupté*. His view of these matters begins in a sort of ecstatic sensuous melancholy, *sons et parfums, sanglots*, intoxicating lashes from the whip of pleasure;[4] dies down into *recueille-*

1. See p. 198.
2. See p. 18.
3. and cf. Ch. II, Ex. 15.
4. ' Sous le fouet du Plaisir, ce bourreau sans merci ' (*Recueillement*).

ment; and finds its quietus not in a religious love-death re-union, but in *La mort des amants:*

> Un soir fait de rose et de bleu mystique,
> Nous échangerons un éclair unique,
> Comme un long sanglot, tout chargé d'adieux;
>
> Et plus tard un Ange, entr'ouvrant les portes,
> Viendra ranimer, fidèle et joyeux,
> Les miroirs ternis et les flammes mortes.[1]

A lovers' disembodiment and apotheosis less grand and uplifting could hardly be imagined.

The progress of Debussy's songs, after this *recueillement* and *mort des amants,* is a gradual sublimation from melancholy voluptuousness to 'fastidious austerity'.[2] As the *Tristan*-side of Debussy fades (the opera where the erotic and the love-death metaphor are celebrated without inner reservation), the *Parsifal*-side (the opera which deals unequivocally and fully with a *conflict* between sexuality and chastity) takes on ever greater significance. Though the sublimation is gradual, the result shows itself ultimately to be a reaction against the 'excesses' of the *Tristan*-style, and if the Verlaine couplet can stand as harbinger of the early Wagnerian works, the motto that lies beyond the late ones could well be Debussy's final search for 'la chair nue de l'émotion'.[3] These final austerities are already presaged in *La Damoiselle élue,* a work in direct contact with *Parsifal. La Damoiselle* has great significance in Debussy's oeuvre; it is the first work in which he grasped 'what he was best suited to do'[4], and thus the first work which indicates the central line of his future development; and also it is the first work in which his idiosyncratic, rather than his conventional, French way of being Wagnerian really tells. Deeply-tinged though it is in *Parsifal,* its Wagnerism is also paradoxically an indication

1. One night — a night of mystic blue, of rose—
   A look will pass supreme from me, from you,
   Like a long sob, laden with long adieux.
   And, later on, an angel will unclose
   The door, and, entering joyously, re-light
   The tarnished mirrors and the flames blown to the night.
   (translated by 'Michael Field').
2. See p. 47.
3. 'How much has to be explored, and discarded, before one can reach the naked flesh of emotion' — Debussy apropos the Sonata for flute, viola and harp.
4. See p. 48.

of the way its composer, in very especial and peculiar ways, is able to transcend yet still contain, the influence of Wagner.

Of course much of the *Damoiselle* attempts simply to do something similar to a Wagnerian original, to approach, like the *Cinq Poèmes,* as near as it can to an aspect of the original's matter and manner. Such things as the 'feathery and swaying voluptuousness' which links the flower-maidens so closely to certain elements in Debussy[1], or the delicate swell of the 'renunciation' motif which so clearly depends from the massive and sonorous deployment of the same idea in *Parsifal*[2] – these show straightforward *influence* (more direct, indeed, than is the norm in the *Cinq Poèmes).* In these instances the subject-matter is the same for both composers, and the younger has learnt directly of the master the musical means for its expression. But already many of the links show the dawning of the Conjunction, where there is that oblique congruity of subject-matter, content, and its musical depiction, which is the very definition of Debussy's Wagnerian works, even though in his first inkling of it, Debussy's treatment naturally cannot sustain any sort of comparison with Wagner's.

The Damozel herself could be described as a Pre-Raphaelite Kundry, rendered undemonic, sexless and bloodless as a creation of Puvis de Chavannes. Kundry has glimpsed but taunted the divine vision, consequently she passes her life seeking redemption down the centuries. She is also Grundygia, the Rose of Hell,[3] possessed by fiendish forces inimical to the holiness she craves. Torn between passionate self-abasement and nymphomaniac abandon, she longs even while she resists Him, for the Redeemer who will resolve her duality and by resisting her lures make her whole. Plainly there is more in this terrific figure than the Damoiselle could, however wanly, reflect. Nonetheless the connection is there – she has her vision, she wavers between wistful chastity, and delicate languishing for the lover who will endorse her in the eyes of the Virgin. But –

–Only to live as once on earth
　　With Love, – only to be,
　As then awhile, for ever now
　　　Together, I and he . . .

1. See Ch. II Ex. 11.
2. See Ch. II, Exx. 2 and 5.
3. Etc.: see *Parsifal* m.s. pp. 350-1.

. . . All this is when he comes . . . .

— this resembles a more disingenuous flower-maiden's seductive appeal, than a call to Christ at once to redeem and to grant the heart's desire. The one factor which distinguishes her from the anonymous *corps de ballet* of Kundry-understudies in *Parsifal* Act II is her self-regard, and in this she is a forerunner of Mélisande. Some parts of the vocal line, and of its relation with a tenuous, evocative orchestral part, can persuade the listener temporarily that it is Mélisande and not the Damozel who sings,[1] so complete is Debussy's sudden emergence into his mature wayward manner. They are alike in their gentle masochism (voluptuous in the earlier case, in the later tending towards a denial of any direct pleasure) and in their narcissism (in the earlier, a tender self-absorption, in Mélisande something, again, which tends towards the denial of human feeling and meaning). But with this exception, the Damozel has hardly progressed beyond the psychological role of a flower-maiden. and neither has her music.

Within the Plot essentially shared between Debussy's opera and *Tristan*, Wagner's subject matter is Passion — 'sensuality . . . unquenchable by any amount of gratification', and Debussy's is 'human loneliness, lack of connection . . . in the end a frigid nihilism'.[2] Debussy's lovers seem as infallibly to find symbols — sleeping paupers, clanking locks, and so forth — for the thwarting of their love, as Isolde and Tristan find the symbols — the shared potion, the torch blazing and quenched — that endorse and give as it were a pretext for their rending of the veil. This was shown most vividly in the comparison of the love-scenes and their respective interruptions, the *Tristan* one horrifying because it breaks into a climax of mutual ecstasy (one is reminded of the Arab, who would prefer to die than be interrupted in the act of love) — whereas the interruption in *Pelléas* comes almost as a relief; so ambiguous has been the relationship, so numb the feeling, that their separation even by Golaud's violent sword is more tolerable than the separateness of the lovers in each other's arms. Moreover Wagner's love-duet interruption, and the scarcely less shattering

1. e.g. m.s. pp. 32-3; 66 to the end.
2. See p. 61.

one in Act III as Isolde arrives and Tristan dies, is eventually healed. Though indeed the heroines of both operas die in the closing pages, Isolde's death-chant and Marke's silent benediction suffuse balm, while Mélisande's silent departure and Arkel's fatalistic closing lines leave only unassuaged anguish.

I have already commented upon the aspects of Debussy's early works which aim to treat Wagnerian matter in a Wagnerian manner. In *Pelléas* the area of this attempt is much diminished, and is also rather different. *La Damoiselle* and particularly the *Cinq Poèmes* showed a genuine correspondence between the original and Debussy's employment of it, whereas in *Pelléas* what was peripheral to Wagner has become central to Debussy. This is a question above all of musical usages, though it is faithfully reproduced in the subject-matter of the Conjunction. Debussy needs to express in music his subject of nihilistic lethargy, and to do this, he has learnt from the prelude of *Tristan* Act III. Similarly, where the music of the early part of Act III of *Parsifal* expresses renunciation and waste, Debussy understands (albeit 'd'une façon impressioniste'), since it fits in with what he, also, wishes to express. Hence his return to this source again and again; it is his richest quarry of musical material in Wagner apart from Kundry and the flower-maidens. But of course the inertia and desolation at the start of the last acts both of *Parsifal* and *Tristan* are temporary, a single stage in complex and arduous journeys towards very different kinds of reconciliation and apotheosis. In *Pelléas* however, inertia and desolation are an unceasing norm; they form a background to the events and characters so all-permeating that it should more aptly be termed the foreground — the listlessness comes forward and swathes the events and characters in itself.

Debussy's discovery that what is central for him in Wagner is in Wagner himself, not exactly peripheral, but one concern among many, implies a further recognition, that what *is* central to Wagner is now too massive for him to deal with, at any rate in direct fashion. His knowledge of his range, and his taste for what suits his particular talents, has extended beyond the range of the earlier Wagnerian works; neither his maturer musical style nor his more developed upper-room manners can by now countenance the characteristic Wagnerian amplitude. This was shown above all in the extraordinary vein of *Tristan*-usages uncovered in section 3 of Chapter VI — 'the *Tristan*-progressions, invented by Wagner to convey enthrallment of a very different kind, are employed by Debussy to circumscribe and colour everything in his drama repressive, inhibitory, harsh and claustrophobic'.[1] This is a more exalted version of an attitude towards the famous motif which the *Golliwogg's Cake Walk* presents with wry and equivocal dislike.[2] No doubt the one is as unconscious as the other is flamboyant, but both provoke the same reaction — they enforce realization that this is an attempt on Debussy's part deliberately *to go against* Wagner — the only instances where his music in some degree bears out his verbal utterances on the subject.

Of the lovers in Debussy's opera the man is timorous and self-deceived, the woman narcissistic and unpossessable, yet at once flirtatious and vulnerable. It has already emerged in this redis-cussion of *La Damoiselle* that Mélisande in certain aspects resembles a Kundry demoted to the flower-maiden ranks, while Chapter IV has examined the curious means whereby Debussy's heroine, corresponding in plot to Isolde, can actually be more closely identified in psychological role to her maid and confidante. So far as the Wagnerian aspect of the music goes, *Parsifal* is evoked for its desolations, *Tristan* for its desolations also, as well as for oblique depictions of repressive miseries.[3] The general effect of Debussy's opera, so far as its relation to Wagner goes, is to bring out in the central relationship and in every peripheral part the essential subject-matter of sadness, lack of fulfillment, lack of meaning both in the microcosm of individual affairs and in the human condition at large.

Tristan of course presents triumphantly the opposite of these fatalisms and nihilisms. Courage and self-knowledge in the man, in the woman soulful self-yielding and self-oblivious submission; out of their mutuality comes fulfillment that is more than human — heroic, and at once tragically purgative and religiously comforting. *Tristan* is the central work for the celebration of passion, sensuality, death-devotion; a vast and astonishingly audacious extension of the traditional conceit of dying in the climax of love. From the

1. See p. 131.

2. See Note, p. 142.

3. Glancing inflections of Norns, Hagen and Hunding, are left to their proper place in Chapter VI.

213

drinking of the death-love potion onwards this conceit swells in a synaesthesia where not only the evidence of our senses but our intellectual-spiritual-physical orientation is blurred and finally abandoned. The consummation of love is interrupted once by an alien festivity, again by treachery and the dawning of the treacherous day, and a third time by the death of the man, who suspires breathing Isolde's name as if in amorous intoxication. She compensates amply in her final celebration over his body; cheated of sexual completion, the lovers cheat death of his expected annihilation. The physical deaths in *Tristan* do not signify as such, for they are Love-Deaths, which stand for sexual completion, and in which the lovers unite in a consciousness transcending the mere exigencies of physical reality. The need to create such a thing as this, the astonishing inspiration and mastery of it as created, the profundity of the pleasure which it, once created, can give to so many people, touches upon psychopathologies so peculiar that an explanation can hardly be envisaged. Christian apotheosis has been fused with Greek catharsis. Purgation desolates and empties; apotheosis avoids the desolation by not enforcing upon the audience a sense of pity and terror — it sends the audience away comforted. *Tristan,* in the death of the hero, and the death-celebration of the heroine, offers catharsis and apotheosis in one. Wagner's purging and elevating force is, quite simply, the music itself; these shocking events, the deaths of the lovers, are rendered bearable even by the medium which expresses them with the greatest intensity; the same medium also conveys in the most rich and direct way possible the redemption of the lovers, and their final bliss.

Wagner's 'enough' is often found to be 'too much'; Debussy in comparison has all the uncertainty of *not enough*. For if *Tristan* is the perfection of fullness and fulfillment, *Pelléas* is surely the perfection of emptiness and attrition. Just as the fullness of music in *Tristan* is the means not only of sparing its audience the painfulness of unadorned catharsis, but also of giving embodiment to the subject-matter which the work expresses, so the 'absence' of music in *Pelléas,* its refusal to celebrate an apotheosis or, except in the most choked manner, to embody anything rich, expresses the essential 'absence' in its subject-matter. Because Debussy's manner is to denude his events and emotions, he in fact succeeds in expressing them with painful and uncomforted intensity. Not insupportably raw and violent as Wagner would be without music, but merely excruciating; a poignancy that can barely articulate itself. The outstanding instance of this is Golaud's 'oh . . . . oh . . .' at Melisande's death;[1] as the *Liebestod* is the highpoint of Wagner's manner of comforting amplitude, so this 'oh . . . oh' is just short of a *reductio ad absurdum* of Debussy's manner of pitiful restraint. The height of excruciation is the nadir of musical content.

A phrase like this recalls the dissatisfactions with *Pelléas* voiced at the end of Chapter VI, which must now be considered further. They are two, that its 'incompatibilities and uncertainties of style reveal a serious incompatibility and uncertainty at the very heart' of the work;[2] and that 'to achieve the perfection of wanness and thinness is less exalted a goal than the achievement of richness and bloom'.[3]

The answer to these dissatisfactions would seem to be absurdly simple. To use Rolland's phrase again, Debussy's music displays such a 'genius for good taste' that, politely avoiding questions or objections which happen to be raised, it effaces itself to the point almost of vanishing. This is not intended to be a frivolous evasion of the difficulties in evaluating *Pelléas*. On the contrary; if the context of suggestion that by now surrounds the mention of Debussy's artistic manners, his idea of civilization, his having a predilection for what suits him — in a word, his taste — has any substance, it should be clear that this is the only way the question can be approached. The whole case is suggested in the phrase 'genius for good taste'; and it contains the explanation of *Pelléas*'s ability successfully to survive in a Conjunction with Wagner, where any straightforward comparison would deprive it of most of its resources. For thinness, emptiness, even 'the nadir of musical content', are obviously in the consideration of Debussy at large and especially in the context of *Pelléas*, by no means pejorative terms. I have called the work the perfection of nihilism; few operas manifest a greater unity of atmosphere, or a more consistent appropriateness of music to subject and story. In its ability effortlessly to touch upon what is elusive, mysterious, quietly disquieting, *Pelléas* is without rival. The technical means whereby it ac-

1. M.s. p. 406.
2. See p. 141.
3. See p. 140.

complishes this magic, however, remain entirely within the pale of Edmund Gurney's dictum by which 'the definiteness in form which first-rate music presents to the hearing ear is compatible with a sense of mystery and infinity which no vagueness can emulate . . .'. Its formlessness is its form, its evasions are its presentations, its uncertainties and incompatibilities its consistencies and rightnesses; its bloom is its wanness, its richness its poverty. Above all, its nihilism and emptiness, words which the discussion of *Pelléas* in its connection to Wagner has so frequently called forth, must be revalued in the light of the Conjunction. They stand for something else; they are Debussy's manner of being full, profound, significant; as the kind of artist he is seen to be, according to the idea of artistic manners he is seen to hold.

It is the peculiar triumph of style in Debussy's opera that it manifests the felicity of imitative form rather than its fallacy. Music in *Pelléas* fades beneath the oppressive yet weightless anguish of the characters; occasionally at the most miserably nihilistic moments it all but disappears; and the nothingness which the opera is quintessentially concerned with is inherent in every moment of the music which accompanies it. 'Imitative form' literally understood would of course mean that a musical depiction of nothing would actually *be* nothing — but here too Debussy's 'genius for good taste' has shown him exactly the right point at which an artistic simulacrum of monotony is prevented actually from being monotonous. One may feel that Satie in *Socrate* has overrated the threshold beyond which boredom ceases to be 'mysterious and profound'; while it is certain that for Cage and Feldman, and in some works of Stockhausen, the possibility of boredom — and hence of interest — has ceased to count as a criterion. Debussy's civilization, taste, and artistic good manners allow him to touch the brink of monotony, to obtain the just amount for his purposes, without stepping beyond. Cage is happy for music to consist of the chaos of noise surrounding our daily lives; other, purer spirits would like music to consist entirely of silence, or a single week-sustained chord (in the regrettable impracticality and expense of infinity); in as much as musical composition is still comprised in the art of combining precisely-notated sounds for well-defined expressive and pleasurable ends, there has to be something on the page. This artistic and expressive minimum, so subtle and potent in its effect, Debussy has achieved: could Mallarmé himself have done less?

It is extraordinary to see that this is, theoretically, the ultimate realization of the Wagnerian principle,[1] though in order to understand its true relation to Wagner *Pelléas* has to be seen as the reversal of everything understood by Wagner's comprehensive art.

My complaint that long stretches of *Le Martyre* were 'simply empty of any significant content'[2] means, in the present context, that they are empty even of significant emptiness. 'Forced to make a comparison between the genuine original and its inferior imitation'[3], Debussy misses the precarious balance of his 'genius for good taste'. Instead, Wagnerian matter and manner are attempted without a due regard for the limitations of his predilections. For such an artist it is impossible, or at least not wise — *tasteless* in a word — to essay subjects and manners which take him outside their range.

The common subject-matter of *Le Martyre* belonging to the Conjunction is the 'kind of voluptuary longing for pain that receives its expression and its quietus in redeeming the guilty from their guilt'.[4] The Saint in *Le Martyre* has the dual role that this implies — on the one side, that of a man consumed like Amfortas by guilt and suffering, on the other, of the *Erlöser* who holds like Parsifal the power to draw unto himself the sufferer's anguish and guilt. Of the first half of this duality the wounded Tristan of Act III is the prototype. His torment stands behind the more morbid and masochistic anguish of Amfortas both psychologically and in musical expression; indeed at an early stage of the *Tristan*-draft the tormented hero was to have been visited by Parsifal in the course of his wanderings, who would presumably have attempted to give him the same balsam that he was able finally to deliver Amfortas. *Tristan* as it now stands has no *Erlöser* — the conflicts externalized and given almost allegorical quality in the later work are, in the earlier, largely submerged and wholly internal.

Longing for pain, and a voluptuary pleasure in both the pain

1. See Chapter III.
2. See p. 148.
3. See p. 147.
4. See p. 145.

and the longing, has emerged as a latent though recognizable theme in all Debussy's Wagnerian works. Beginning in the conventional French background of pleasure – *extase* and 'all that thrills' – it received luscious expression in the Baudelaire songs while contemporaneously the first example of its more characteristically Debussyan version, the tenderly vulnerable Damoiselle, was being composed. Mélisande and Pelléas in their different ways greatly extend what the Damoiselle implies, while Golaud becomes an unexpectedly urgent depiction of sado-masochism, admittedly in a tradition of character-portrayal alien to Wagner, though shot through with recollections of Tristan, Klingsor, Hunding and Hagen.

'Masochism' is something of a simplistic usage here – for the Debussyan tendency the word is too strong, and for the Wagnerian it is too incomplete. To describe Tristan and Amfortas as manifesting simply masochistic emotions would be an absurd distortion. Both characters are psychological studies of searching and disquieting profundity; longing for pain is only one element in the complex gamut of interrelated emotions that they cover. Nevertheless of the two, Amfortas approaches more nearly to an 'exposition' of masochism than Tristan, and it is the role of Amfortas, and his music, from which the music and role of Sébastien are derived.

Amfortas's torment is given something of its true dimension in some remarks of Friedrich von Hügel on pain; '– that real pain which comes ready to our hand for turning into the *right* pain – gets offered us by God . . .' and his prescription for how to suffer it and gain from the suffering:-

> . . . try more and more, at the moment itself, without any delay or evasion, without any fixed form, as simply, as spontaneously as possible, to cry out to God, to Christ our Lord, . . . 'oh! oh! This is real . . . oh may this pang deepen me, may it help to make *me* real – really humble, really loving, really ready to live or die with my soul in thy hands'.

Evidently the mechanism provided by von Hügel, pure and disinterested as it is, need not be taken much further to reach a state of masochistic rapture. An element of pain-loving is surely present in Amfortas; contemplating the heights and depths to which he flagellates himself in his desire for purity, we hear in his music a

218

gloomy Nordic counterpart (for Monsalvat's geographical setting
is a mere castle in Spain) to the amorous agonies of a St Theresa
— violent and hyper-dissonant, but still imbued with the carnal
fervour for which his flesh now atones.

Debussy's native ideal of pleasure is in turn given its true dimension (in a passage of didactic exegesis alien, admittedly, to his
manners) in the traditional Epicurean ideal:-

When we are pained because of the absence of pleasure, then,
and then only do we feel the need of pleasure. Wherefore we
call pleasure the alpha and omega of a blessed life. Pleasure is
our first and sovereign good. It is the starting-point of every
choice and of every aversion, and to it we come back, inasmuch
as we make feeling the rule by which to judge of every good
thing . . . And oft times we consider pains superior to pleasures
when submission to the pains for a long time brings us as a
consequence a greater pleasure. While therefore all pleasure
because it is naturally akin to us is good, not all pleasure is
choiceworthy, just as all pain is an evil and yet not all pain is
to be shunned.

Amfortas's experience of pain, as clarified by von Hügel, turns
into a kind of pleasure; while the hedonist experience of pleasure
which might be offered as the rationale of Debussy's attitude, is
intimately linked with the experience of pain. It takes Debussy, as
the child of his time and place (post-Baudelairean, mid-Wagnerian
Paris) and the willing slave of his predilections, to merge the two.
Amfortas feels the flesh burning in the spirit; he says in effect, 'I
welcome my agony, dear God! because by making my wound burn
you bring me closer to purgation; you lacerate the part of me
which perpetually reminds me of my sin; through my consciousness
of my pain I come closer to you'. Such pain, though an evil, is not
to be shunned; voluptuary relish of bodily agony is transformed
into spiritual release. In Debussy's and d'Annunzio's amorous
Epicureanism however, the masochist feels the flesh burning in
itself; the words 'oh! this is real . . . oh may this pang deepen me,
may it help to make *me* real . . .' become unambiguously erotic,
the lover's pinch that hurts and is desired, voluptuousness driven
beyond pleasure into pain for the intensification of pleasure. The
vulgarity of *Le Martyre* consists in its taking crude advantage of
these subtly shifting loyalties. The saint's unctuous religious

fervour rides under the sting of 'le fouet du plaisir'. All in all, when the allurements of the Crucifixion, mimed by a sensual Jewish tragedy-queen ('I kiss your bleeding legs', telegrammed d'Annunzio to Ida Rubinstein) – are borne in mind, *Le Martyre* would seem to be another instance of Nietzsche's words fitting better a work of Debussy than the Wagner work from which it derives and about which they were first written: *Le Martyre*, much more than *Parsifal*, is a 'mere vehicle for the psychologically picturesque'.

As with the earlier comparison of Mélisande and the Damoiselle to a Kundry made flower-maiden, there is here the feeling that the possible parallels between such originals as Amfortas and Parsifal and such an echo of them as Sébastien must seem pretty tightly-stretched. Not that the resemblance is not obvious; but because the originals are so tremendous and the echo so shadowy and uncreated that there can be no enlightenment in solemnly weighing the one against the other and deciding that Debussy has the disadvantage. Yet his final attempt at Wagnerian matter and 'lower-room' manner is significant beyond its inevitable failure. The theme is clearly an important part of the Conjunction, and some kind of direct assault upon it was probably necessary before it could be assimilated, and pass through leaving not a wrack behind.

The special significance of *Jeux* is that it gathers up every element in the Debussy-Wagner Conjunction and, for a moment, holds them in a synthesis: all the aspects I have isolated in the earlier works, musical and psychological, are present, either directly or by subtle and even devious implication; and are treated in the shortest space and with the richest working.

In the midst of this general synthesis there are two works which enjoy a particular closeness of relation. With *Le Martyre* it is a case of literal musical influence; it was written the year before *Jeux*, and in it all kinds of discoveries which came to their full bloom there, seem to be essayed for the first time. The fast part of the 'Danse extatique de Sébastien sur les charbons embrasés' in the 1st Mansion is a diluted version of the more fluttery-motioned, just as its languid section is of the marvellously rich slow parts, of Debussy's ballet. The *femmes de Byblos* mourn their – shall we say? – Adonis/Sébastien/Christ/Parsifal with sinuous flower-maid lines, the orchestra supporting them with parallel and contrary-motion chromatic chords compounded in somewhat unequal measure of grief and amorous longing. *Jeux* intensifies the aura of masochistic lusciousness in *Le Martyre,* and the musical resemblance between this aspect of the two scores, coming down sometimes to specific harmonic, melodic, and orchestral details, is striking.[1]

The other special relationship is between *Jeux* and *L'après-midi d'un faune,* and here there is a proximity of events if not of composition. Nijinsky had choreographed *L'après-midi* for Diaghilev earlier in the same year that *Jeux* was written, and made of the title-role what is nowadays commonly claimed to be one of his most spectacularly beautiful parts (though the composer himself disliked the Eurythmic influence in the choreography). A well-known scandal arose because Nijinsky's interpretation made explicit the latent eroticism of Mallarmé's original poem as well as Debussy's music to it. That *L'après-midi* was in the air (with a *frisson* of 'naughtiness') in May 1912, and that *Jeux,* completed that autumn, was composed for the same dancer and company, cannot be without significance. I do not postulate specific musical connections — rather, that the fortuitous linking of the latest work with the work of the early 1890s has the effect, which might otherwise be more difficult to observe, of focusing what they have in common.

The subject-matter (if it can still be called that) of *L'après-midi* is imbued with a lascivious sun-basking quality; it lingers on the fantasy rather than the act of love, then lingers in nostalgia for its own velleity; it urges the directness of masculine sensuality, muted by being only a dream, and expressed with all the *chaleurs* and subtleties 'from the vocabulary of happiness'. By forcing the covert into the blatant, Nijinsky reduced the thrilling *pudeurs* of *L'après-midi* to something approaching the *risqué* 'idiocy'[2] of the *Jeux*-scenario. The link can be made most succinctly by calling *L'après-midi* the nineteenth-century *Jeux* and *Jeux* the twentieth-

---

1. Cf. *Le Martyre* m.s. *(Fragments Symphoniques)* — 36 — 'Je danse sur l'ardeur des lys' with *Jeux* m.s. pp. 38-9; 42-3. Arabesque plaint of the Women of Byblos, *Le Martyre* v.s. p. 55f. *Jeux*-like rhythm and luscious parallel and contrary-motion chords, *Le Martyre* v.s. pp. 57-8; 60; 68-9 (scoring given in *Fragments Symphoniques* p. 61).

2. See p. 160.

century *Faune. Jeux* also has its single male and its several nymphs; it presents the violence of the daydreams in the earlier work, as well as their lascivious character, with much greater sharpness and wealth of detail; as also their climax and rapid evanescence.

But there is more to the connection than this. Just as *L'après-midi* more than any other work of Debussy had been the Open Sesame to the avant-garde musicians of its day — 'the music made an extraordinary and indefinable impression on me, like a fantastic world perceived for the first time'[1] — so *Jeux* more than any other work of Debussy has been the inspiration of two generations of mid-twentieth-century composers of many different tendencies. And as far as my particular interest here is concerned, *L'après-midi* represents a synthesis of Debussy's earlier Wagnerian works, both in subject and in musical style — a synthesis in which, foreshadowing the later one of *Jeux,* the overt presence of the original is hardly any more to be traced. It would be all very well to point out that the very first chord in *L'après-midi* is 'the *Tristan*-chord' and to proceed from there. The point is, that the loss of specific Wagnerian usage in a general Wagnerian *suffusion* that was first noticed in *La mort des amants*[2] has in *L'après-midi* gone so much further that there is nothing analytic to be said about it. It is a prototype of the final Wagnerian connection which leaves 'not the cluttered débris of an influence, but a diaphony radically original, though everywhere suffused with what has passed through'.[3]

What *L'après-midi* performed for the comparatively straightforward relation of Debussy's early works to Wagner, *Jeux* does for the idiosyncratic and difficult relation to Wagner manifested in Debussy's later and greater works. Chapter VIII detailed the extraordinary manner in which Debussy's last orchestral score is a sort of suspension, 'by subtle association, by delicate assimilation,'[4] of the subject-matter and music of *Parsifal* as a whole. I have tried here to bring together the more complex currents which also find their moment of convergence in this work. As *L'après-midi* is Debussy's happiest response to *Tristan,* so *Jeux* is *Parsifal* as it must appear in the upper room, stripped of ideas, plot, symphony, masculine weight and German sublimity. Emptied too of meaning;

1. Casella's autobiography *Music in my Time.* His reaction is representative.

2. See p. 44.

3. See p. 192.

4. See p. 192.

but not, like *Pelléas,* finding this to be of necessity an attrition, a denial of vitality, abundance, pleasure. Nor is it meaning-*less,* simply 'not meaning*ful*'; it holds its significances deep in its ravishing surfaces. Both works are hedonistic, dealing with the senses rather than the sensibilities, with empirical rightness rather than classical correctness. They show the delights of the Debussy-Wagner Conjunction at their richest and most profound. After the first came the desolations of subject and the thinning of music of *Pelléas;* after the later work, the failure of the hedonist ideal, and the reversion to formality (a formality as fugitive and excentric as might be expected) and the 'chair nue de l'émotion'. Above all, beyond the perfection of form-to-content and content-to-form which they share, *L'après-midi* and *Jeux* have a wonderful bloom (inexplicable to analysis, which cannot account for any merely technical difference between a work which is felt to have it and one that lacks it); a lustre of depth and surface, that glow of artistic health indicating the work's substance to be in every respect in felicitous correlation with what its creator is gifted to do, and desires to.

The relation to Wagner can for a moment become pure metaphor:-

. . . for all other rivers there is a surface, and an underneath, and a vaguely displeasing idea of the bottom. But the Rhône flows like one lambent jewel; its surface is nowhere, its ethereal self is everywhere, the iridescent rush and translucent strength of it blue to the shore and radiant to the depth.

5. *En Plus*

The position by now is as follows. On the one side Wagner — to be sure, only that aspect (a central one however) which signifies for Debussy. His manner one of repletion, richly-upholstered heights and depths; behind him the ample resources of German melody, harmony, counterpoint, orchestra, and architecture. The aspect which matters for Debussy is Wagner's supremely expressive treatment of the conflict between sacred and profane. *Tristan* presents it under the auspices of the Erotic — a classic instance of the type of 'Demonic Man' — 'Demonic indeed seems the abyss which cannot be filled, the yearning which cannot be assuaged, the thirst which cannot be slaked'.[1] *Parsifal* is Wagner's attempt to fill, assuage, and slake; an answer to *Tristan,* growing out of it in musical language as well as subject (though *Tristan* had itself originated as an emanation of the initial idea for *Parsifal).* Here the conflict between flesh and spirit is treated in a manner so thorough-going as to make the work, with *Comus* and *Clarissa* and certain writings of St Paul, a central treatment of the subject. And just as the Erotic in *Tristan* tended towards expression in terms of religious devotion, so the spiritualities of *Parsifal* tend towards expression in terms of the voluptuous.

This is the *fons et origo* of Debussy's Wagnerian works: the flow between it and them is summarized as follows. The expression in *Pelléas* of desolate nihilism comes from the opening reaches of the final Acts both of *Parsifal* and of *Tristan.* The hedonist vein begins in raptures learnt from *Tristan* Act II and flirtations and *frissons* learnt from Act II of *Parsifal.* The strain of voluptuous masochism, at first a specialized side-stream from the ideal of pleasure, later makes a surprising sally towards the areas of experience touched on in Tristan's Act III monologue and fully explored in Amfortas. The preceding sections of this chapter have detailed the interconnections of these relationships; and after the synthesis in *Jeux,* in which the weight of all these Wagnerian themes is treated with manners of such astonishing levity, the Wagnerian content in Debussy disappears. Stravinsky's remarks about the Italianate melodic element in Wagner come to mind, which 'curls through the whole of his music from *Das Liebesverbot* to *Parsifal* (and on to *Verklärte Nacht*) without ever being digested'.[2] Debussy, on the contrary, succeeds in digesting the Wagnerian elements in his style — though digestion is too gross an image for the relation between the luminous bed and crystalline surface of the Rhône. After *Jeux* come the Mallarmé settings, the sudden resurgence of a wholly unWagnerian opulence in the *Etudes,* and the austerities and limpidities of the sonatas and *En blanc et noir.* Debussy's hedonism, beginning in 'mon plaisir', after a lifetime of involvement with a version of the Erotic so much more powerful and intoxicating than his own, compels it to sub-

---

1. Quoted from Zeigler: *Das Heilige Reich der Deutschen* (1925) in Lotte Eisner's book on the expressionist film.

2. *Themes and Conclusions* p. 246: from a review of a volume of Wagner's prose.

mit, and allow him the Pyrrhic triumph of the freedom to behave entirely according to his own manner.

This simplistic formula is emphatically not offered as a distillation of the Debussy-Wagner Conjunction; *that* only exists in as much as it is a maze of suggestive details. However I am now at that point where, like Pope, it is necessary to choose whether my maze is 'not without a plan' or 'all without a plan'.[1] But before concluding, I would like to explore two speculations which do tend to spoil the neatness of the Conjunction.

The first is a suggestion that the central conflict in *Parsifal* is symbolized in the music at its broadest by the contrast between diatonic 'purity' and chromatic 'evil'. In *Tristan* the contrast had been a simple one, the occasional diatonic sailors' chorus or a motif like Kurwenal's standing out as islands in the ubiquitous surges of chromaticism. In *Parsifal* diatonicism has more equal representation. Under it come Parsifal's own motif, the motif of the Grail, the Dresden Amen, the Act I processional music, the pentatonic bells, the healing influences of nature — everything implicit in the diatonic intervals of the opening statement of the opening theme. Under the other there is the sickening chromatic see-saw of Klingsor's motifs, the iridescent shiftings of the flower-maidens and Kundry, and the agonies of Amfortas — everything implied by the chromatic intervals introduced with an effect of stabbing dissonance even in the unison second statement of the opening theme. Act I for all its exceptions is fundamentally the act of diatonicism; Act II of chromaticism entirely. The early reaches of Act III show the chromaticism yet more intense, but at the same time wearied and washed-out.[2] After the serene diatonicism of the Good Friday flowers (with passing chromatic memories of the evil flowers of Act II), the second transformation and procession music, expressing the Brotherhood's despair at the loss of their leader, anguish at their deprivation of the healing graces of the Grail, shame at the ruin of their Order, and bitter condemnation of Amfortas as the author of these woes, contain some of the most tortuous chromatic harmony ever written that is still encompassed within tonal usage. This in turn (after further extension by Amfortas himself) gives way in the final apotheosis to the work's most radiant diatonic paragraphs.

1. *An Essay on Man* 1:6. (the former eventually stood).
2. Cf. Wagner's description, pp. 165 - 6.

Already the discussion of *La Damoiselle* implied a latent contrast between the diatonics and lilies of virtue and the chromatics of rapturous yearning. Indeed the enchanting little work encompasses the same duality, and the shifting area between the opposites, of the enormous masterpiece from which it depends; and with the same intention of meaning. The *Tristan*-saturated *Cinq Poèmes*, as befits their subject-matter, are highly chromatic throughout. In discussion of *Pelléas* the Russian influence introduced a breath of diatonic air into the mournful atmosphere of constraints derived from *Tristan* and desolations remembered from *Parsifal*. Mussorgsky in particular gives Debussy 'the language of lyricism and freshness . . . as if neither gaiety and innocence on the one hand, nor on the other passion however grave, could be rendered by Debussy with any elements of Wagnerian vocabulary'.[1] But the diatonic pastoral music in *Le Martyre* is a feeble re-hash of earlier felicities; the score's memorable parts are first, the highly chromatic souvenir of the first *Parsifal* transformation music,[2] and secondly the diatonic choruses whose white purity is inspired by the effect of the choral element in Wagner's opera, rather than influenced by its substance.[3] And *Jeux* disposes with a pirouette of discussion which would seek to imbue the very elements of music with moral qualities — for *Jeux* (as *L'après-midi*, much more simply, had also been) is by turns highly chromatic and very diatonic.

For all the variety of genre in Debussy's oeuvre as a whole, there remain common stylistic features which give it its striking particularity; one of the most important of these is his employment of chromatic and diatonic as, with the greater weakening of tonal usage, a sort of polarity. His diatonicism tends towards the pentatonic (for instance, *Pagodes),* his chromaticism towards the whole-tone (for instance, *Cloches à travers les feuilles); Voiles* is a famous instance of the juxtaposition of pure whole-tone writing with pure pentatonicism. Of course it would be fanciful to suggest that the especially close blend of chromatic and whole-tone with pentatonic and diatonic in *Jeux* is still further evidence of the work's reduction of 'the richness of psychological meaning and musical material in all three acts of *Parsifal.*'[4] Rather, its synthesis

1. See p. 139.
2. See Ch. VII Ex. 2a and b.
3. See pp. 157 - 8.
4. See p. 159.

and concentration of so many aspects of his own style makes an additional reason for its supreme position in the Debussyan canon. But a general point, not pressed beyond its limits, is perhaps valid, that the suggestive power for expression of the diatonic-chromatic contrast in Wagner is reflected, according to the idiosyncratic workings of their Conjunction, in both the musical material and the subject-matter of the appropriate works of Debussy.

My second simplified speculation returns once more to the declaration that 'the music of *Jeux* is inseparable from the subject-matter, which is sexual pleasure'; and its intention (in spite of appearances) is to effect a still more complete immersion into the substance of the music. It is a question of the extent to which music can be a metaphor for, or a simulacrum of, the varieties of sexual experience which are its subject-matter.

Wagner of course has treated the subject comprehensively and explored it to the limits of its meaning. The whole range — from the first breath which troubles the heavens, through increase of desire into yearning, through sexual pleasures and the intoxications of sensuality, through interruptions which deepen and sharpen the desire, to eventual fulfilment; and beyond it to sexual guilt, the sense of what Wagner called 'Liebe als Qual'; to an eventual renunciation, a sublimation of the whole area which loses not an iota of the chalorous power of every preceding stage — all this is present. The manner of his music in treating this matter: a wave-formation, swelling and relapsing, heaving and subsiding, higher and more ecstatically-charged with each renewed assault. The music becomes a metaphor for the body's raptures as of the motions of these raptures in the mind, tumescence and detumescence writ in the consciousness at large.

Vaulty, voluminous . . . stupendous,
it strains to be our love, our sensuality, our death. It 'dismembers and disremembers' us as it enforces our participation in its motion. It 'whelms, whelms and will end us' — in *Tristan* with its oceanic 'mingling of voluptuousness and anguish in which the souls, eager to melt into one another, encountered the impenetrable obstacle of the body' — eroticism of body and soul at once; in *Parsifal* with its thrill after thrill of ever more debilitating psychological seduction — 'something experienced in the very depths of music' —

spiritual fervour at once soulful and carnal.[1] The music does more than express all this; it stands for it as a metaphor: the plot and subject-matter are the music's *raison d'être,* but it is the music which gives them not only their potency of expression, but their *être* itself. In as much as such a statement can be made, these things are the *meaning* and *content* of all the complex of technicalities which make up the actual appearance of the printed page and the sound of it when performed.

Debussy's music offers something nearer still to the subject: its content and meaning, for all the manifold sophistications of its technical aspect, comes down to something approaching an imitation of its particular version of sexual pleasure; and this moreover is the sole intention, as it is the sole effect, of its existence. His manner is perfectly in accordance with what is expected in the upper room. Where Wagner is explicit, Debussy implies; Wagner will sway whomsoever he desires to whether or not they are willing, while only those subtly attuned to his style can collaborate with Debussy in the full expression of shared predilections. Debussy's music echoes the swell and fall of Wagner's but with a certain sharp, unrounded quality – it is altogether shorter-breathed, human in scale rather than gigantic. Wagnerian culmination is ample and prolonged; the climax overwhelming, resolving enormous tensions; and the music sinks satisfied and quiescent, still rich and full, but with the blandness of repletion. Debussy shows a less idealistic, much more directly physical apprehension; his culminations become ever faster, thinner, more febrile; no *sostenuto;* and after so brief and intense an arrival, an immediate deflation, regret, limp poignancy, disengagement, silence – the composer's so-characteristic 'inclinaison pudique vers le bas'.[2] And if Wagner interrupts his culminations, both the physical in *Tristan* and the psychological in *Parsifal,* in order to defer satisfaction and achieve fulfilment on a spiritual rather than an erotic level, Debussy allows an interruption only to a fantasy, or only after everything is achieved; the *voyeur* at the end of *Jeux* dissipates the nostalgic, fleeting afterpleasures rather than interrupt the game itself.

1. The first quotation is from the *Tristan*-chapter in d'Annunzio's *Triumph of Death;* for the second see p.16 ; the general imagery of the paragraph comes from Hopkins's sonnet *Spelt from Sibyl's Leaves.*

2. Jankélévitch: *Debussy et le Mystère,* cited by Lockspeiser.

Objections

Put more soberly, Wagner's musical motion achieves an erotic swell, varying in intensity from placid to frenzied but always effecting a sequentially overpowering yet at the same time predictable 'machine-made' incandescence: while Debussy seems to be employing for his altogether more delicious, less monumental version of the same effect, nothing corresponding to the inner motions of mind and body; only the nerves, only the sense of touch, only what titillates and lightly arouses. Wagner's music is a metaphor for the whole range of emotions involved in the bodily acts; Debussy's is a simulacrum of their whole range of sensation and delight.

6. *Objections*

Now in effecting such extremely delicate overlappings of music and its meanings the danger must be avoided not only of finding what is in dubious taste, but also what is actually not to be found. Stravinsky has some remarks about the interpretative attempt which put the second objection plainly:-

> As I see it, the metaphorical alignments, symbolizations, reflected thoughts and feelings, are purely the listener's, without any 'real' basis in the music; or, in other words, the investing of the musical object with the listener's subjective responses is actually nothing more than a form of the pathetic fallacy.

'For me', Stravinsky adds a little later in the same interview,[1] 'all interest passes to the object, the thing made'.

The neo-classic illusion[2] dies hard! For if it is the precise and deliberate intention of a musical object, a thing made, that it produce certain 'symbolizations, reflected thoughts and feelings' in its hearers, then for them to find these things in the music is not at all a distortion. Rather than reading into the music what is in actuality located in themselves, the hearers' response is appropriate to what, located in the music itself, they are supposed to be responding to. Here subjectivity would be correct — indeed here subjectivity is objective. The older definitions of these somewhat-

1. 'Stravinsky at Eighty-Five', *Themes and Conclusions* pp. 109-10

2. A reminder (continuing the quotation from Stravinsky's *Autobiography* begun p.198): '*Expression* has never been an inherent property of music. That is by no means the purpose of its existence. If, as is nearly always the case, music appears to express something, this is only an illusion and not a reality'. etc.

abused words clarify my anti-purist position. Johnson's Dictionary gives *subjective* as 'relating not to the object but the subject', and *objective* as 'belonging to the object; contained in the object'. Definitions unexceptionable enough! though useful in stripping the words of their modern veneer, where subjective implies 'self-deceived' or '-indulgent' and objective implies 'rational' and 'truthful'. The example given by Johnson, from Isaac Watts, really does forward definition:-

> Certainty, according to the schools, is distinguished into objective and subjective. Objective certainty is when the proposition is certainly true in itself; and subjective, when we are certain of the truth of it. The one is in things, the other in our minds.

In considering the music of Wagner, to take an interest in 'the thing made' must be the same as to respond to the 'metaphorical alignments' that it embodies: they are contained in the object; are certainly true in themselves; and are contained in our own minds, where we are certain of the truth of them. The purity of the anti-interpretative position is specious, for what is made is, exactly, what is meant. 'Pathetic Fallacy No Fallacy' here, at least.

The objection, at first seemingly so damaging, can be disregarded more readily than the sort of demur which goes halfway with and half against a determinedly interpretative approach; this quotation is an example:-

> Music condenses a very large amount of inner life, of the sort of experience which might lend itself to such general associations, into a very brief space of actual time. The succession of intensity and relaxation, the expectation perpetually bred and perpetually satisfied, the constant direction of the motion to new points, and constant evolution of part from part, comprise an immense amount of alternations of posture and of active adjustment of the will. We may perhaps even extend the suggestions . . . so far as to imagine that this ever-changing adjustment of the will, subtle and swift in Music beyond all sort of parallel, may project on the mind faint intangible images of extra-musical impulse and endeavour; and that the ease and spontaneity of the motions, the certainty with which a thing known or dimly divined as about to happen *does* happen, creating a half-illusion that the notes are obeying the controlling force of one's own desire, may similarly open up vague channels of association with

other moments of satisfaction and attainment.

This passage from Edmund Gurney's *The Power of Sound* excites endorsement rather than repudiation. Gurney admits in modest language the possibilities which I would unequivocally declare. When he continues 'But these affinities are at any rate of the most absolutely general kind' I add, yes, usually; but not in the case of a composer who boldly like Wagner invests music with a quasi-semantic meaning, or a composer like Debussy who renders shades of *finesse* whose purpose and effect are very far from those normally understood by 'abstract'. And when Gurney concludes '... whatever their importance may be, (these affinities) seem to me to lie in a region where thought and language struggle in vain to penetrate', I admire the scruple, but am willing to make the attempt — an endeavour neither so courageous nor so foredoomed as it would be if the interpretation of music that patently *is* abstract was my goal. The real vulgarity (to refer back to the opening sentence of this section) would be, to pass by on the other side from the content and subject-matter; where Wagner and Debussy are concerned, the composers' own extra-musical significances (through 'extra' is the opposite of what is really meant) are in active collusion with the interpretative effort.

In fact the serious objection is that the particular affinities and alignments I have offered, rather than offensive or far-fetched, are all too explicit and obvious. The view, in the particular areas of the particular works under consideration, that Wagner's music offers a metaphor for and Debussy's a simulacrum of, the range of feelings and pastimes which centre in sexual pleasure, can as easily obscure illumination and limit the field of understanding as it can open up a new apprehension of how things are. And in addition, to find merely *this* as the quarry and focus of the discussion; *this*, it will be urged, is to reduce complex works of art to something intolerably simple and crude. Further definitions may help to answer this objection. When I say that the music of the Wagner–Debussy Conjunction 'means' (as a metaphor or simulacrum) 'certain kinds of sexual pleasure', what in turn do *I* mean in claiming that it means what I say? 'Anything acquires meaning if it is connected with, or indicates, or refers to, something beyond itself, so that its full nature points to and is revealed in that connection'.[1] And taking it further,[2] '. . . the 'meaning' of a thing is the highest form of its co-existence with other things . . . it is not enough to have the material body of a thing; I need, besides, to know its 'meaning', that is to say, the mystic shadow which the rest of the universe casts upon it'. The condition I postulate is one where music seeks to evoke or stand for the sexuality it expresses: but this is not *simply* what it means, for the sexuality itself stands for 'other things' — it is the 'material body' by which we understand the significances and intensities of which it is an outward and symbolic form. Its meaning is not that of a dehumanized animal activity. On the contrary, its meaning is its power, through the physical passions and their psychological reverberations, to act as a focus of the human comprehension of its own existence. In the Debussy-Wagner Conjunction, sexuality is the central *donnée* which like a magnet sets the drift of the surrounding matter into a coherent pattern. Whatever the ambiguities and 'horrors'[3] of the changing configurations the fundamental loyalty never shifts. 'The degree and kind of a man's sexuality permeate the very loftiest heights of his intellect'.[4]

The objection, here made specially about one point, could be extended to cover the general attempt in this final chapter to describe a significant bond between the two composers. For, as has already been indicated, the end of any series of connections must always be the realization that Debussy and Wagner are two extraordinarily distinct and separate phenomena, in Conjunction only when seen from a rarified and specialized angle. The doubt in a metaphor of this kind is, what can its function be when there is no direct comparison to be made. There is Wagner; there is Debussy: something at once concrete and incommunicable links them together. Is it merely something that they have in common, or do they change under the Conjunction, and become something else in relation to each other? And does such a Conjunction extend or constrict understanding of the two composers it con-

1. M. Cohen, quoted in Epperson, *The Musical Symbol.*

2. Ortega y Gasset.

3. See p. 161.

4. Thomas Mann, quoting Nietzsche apropos of Platen; (*Essays of Three Decades,* p. 265).

cerns? The essence of its implied comparison can be narrowed down to something like this. In some artists (of whom Wagner is a supreme example) the creative impulse originates in a need to understand themselves and a desire to reveal their self-understanding to the world. Whereas the complementary kind of artist (of which Debussy is a supreme example) uses his art to deepen the mystery and keep explicit understanding at bay; and in doing this, he exercises in his work aspects of his personality so fugitive as to be in effect unconscious. The metaphor which conjoins the two sees Debussy as a Wagner repressed by an ideal of fastidious artistic manners; or, the other way round, Wagner as a Debussy who, released from inhibition and false delicacy, allows himself to speak out what is in his mind, without having to have recourse to understatement. The subject-matter is the same for both, though made essentially different by such different ideals of taste and style. The metaphor of their Conjunction would not function if it were merely a verbal connection; as it stands, it both respects the heterogeneity of the two composers, yet finds possibilities for yoking them together in such a way as further to explain them, both individually and in relation to each other.

7. Conclusion

A return to the differences ultimately obtaining between Wagner and Debussy is the point for the final gathering of threads. It must be said again that to present their differences in terms of a *contrast* merely, though of course not untrue, is to militate against the possibilities of understanding them further. Thus, one of the most striking contrasts they present is in terms of artistic fulfilment — Wagner's total performance of everything, unprecedentedly ambitious as it was, that he set out to accomplish, as against Debussy's career, littered with projects abandoned with a sense of almost compulsive inachievement. But to point a contrast like this does nothing to aid understanding of their relation to each other.

Another difference, however, does do just this. As opposed to the 'ample resources of German melody, harmony, counterpoint, orchestra, and architecture' which place Wagner so securely in a great tradition, Debussy stands in a non-tradition, or rather, in a culture where every composer of outstanding gifts has had to 'make it new'. In French music nothing is handed down, every major figure is a law unto himself, without direct ancestry and with progeny only of *pasticheurs*. To solve the problems raised by his own newness, the French composer has to fall back on his interior resources rather than using the accumulated experience of a conventional language. Newness in a conventional language is originality, which expands that language's capacities without vitiating the spirit of its canons. Newness in a history without inherited traditions tends towards the odd or even the grotesque. Hence, it is in these traditionless histories that we find the predilection *avant toute chose* – the special case, the exotic influence, the idiosyncratic 'taste for'; where, rather than a language handed down and constantly developed, we have a series of styles.

Debussy even amongst all his highly-differentiated fellow French composers is so special that it is in fact easier to understand him as a 'mutation' than it is to connect him with his origins. His work has been almost universally understood as being of the essence of the New. While this is true, it nonetheless has the effect slightly of dislocating perception of his relation to the past, of obscuring its importance, and making it difficult to gauge its extent. The old in Debussy is not simply a *point de départ*, but continues to inform the whole journey. My purpose has been to try to show Debussy in this different light; show (within the limits of the title) that for all his manifest originality, much of the profoundity of meaning in his music, as well as many of its linguistic features, come about through the rich elements of the old working in it in secret.

The originality of Debussy is perhaps the most radical break with musical tradition ever made. But in consequence there is something about his newness which in the end compels the acknowledgement of a certain insubstantiality. Much of his work is 'nouveau pauvre'; I coin the phrase to imply not the sudden poverty of an ancient line fallen upon hard times, but as a corollary of *nouveau riche,* something rootless, without endorsement, without standing. Debussy emerges as a greater composer seen as the heir to what he emerges from and implicitly contains. Seen as the harbinger of the avant-garde, he is simply 'significant', or 'interesting' — in a word, a mannerist. Even if the results of his radicality had proved more valuable than has so far emerged, this alone could not be a criterion for his importance. It is hindsight, in fact — a distortion of him just as he distorts Wagner.

Wagner for Debussy is the old; the old in him is his Wagnerian content, contained in the extraordinarily idiosyncratic and suggestive ways that I have attempted to elicit and interpret. Through his Conjunction with Wagner, Debussy is prevented from being merely a mannerist, with the mannerist's disembodiment (for all his interest and significance) from the mainstream of his times. Debussy's possession and transformation of Wagner gives him substantiality, signification, and depth.

Of course Debussy can never be called the heir to Wagner in any traditional sense by which influences are understood to be passed on. Rather than a follower who continues his line, Debussy is Wagnerian in a unique way, standing at an angle to him, in a relation at once factual and ideal. The factual I have documented; the ideal I have attempted to build up through the similarities, antitheses, comparisons, contrasts, and speculations, which make up their Conjunction. In the combination of the two lies my interpretation of the meaning of their connection. The first Chapter ended with an assertion, premature and not a little rash, that Debussy 'must be recognized to be the most Wagnerian of all composers'. It has been my intention gradually in the chapters that intervene to have subtilized the crudity of this initial assertion; so that by the time of its reiteration here it will seem not only to be properly substantiated, but also to possess a certain inevitability.

DATE D